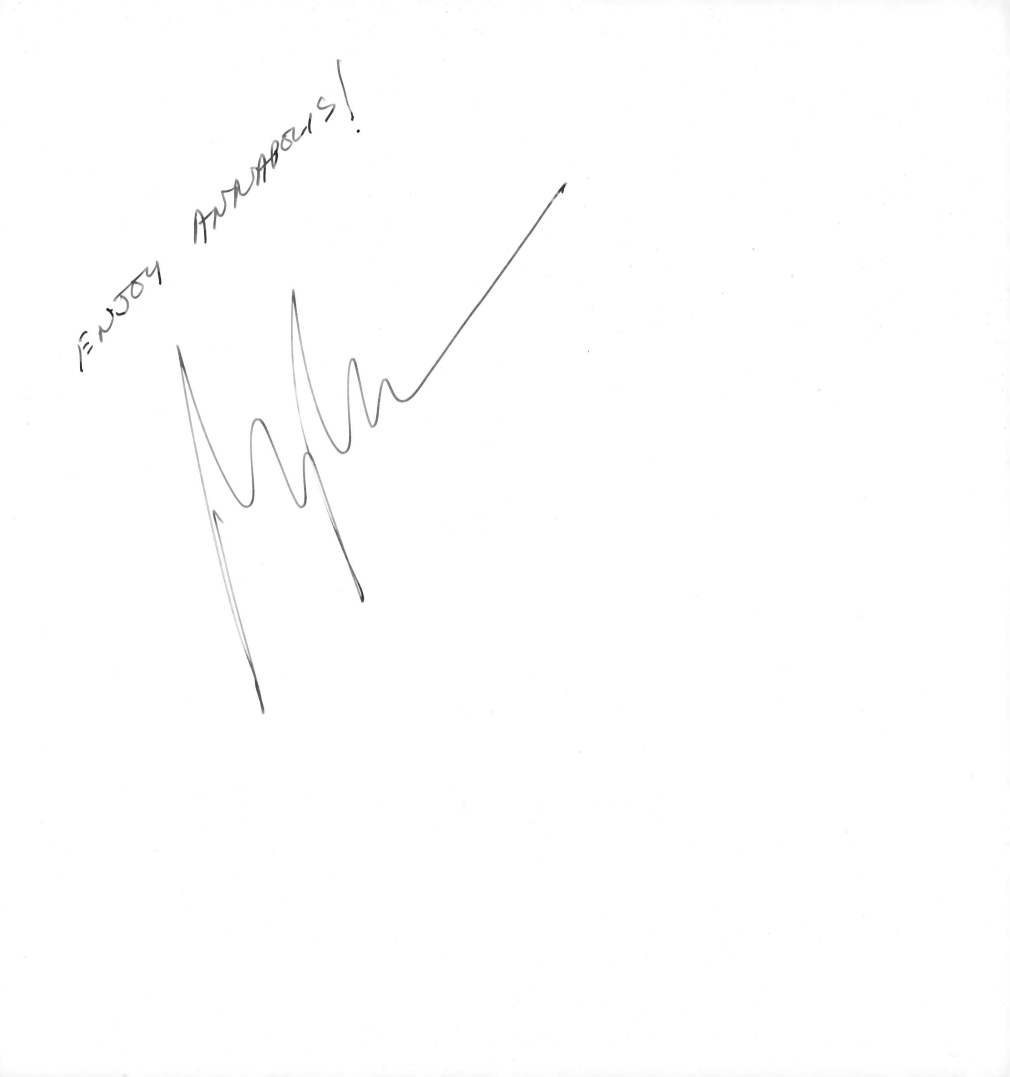

ENJOY ANNAPOLIS!

ANNAPOLIS A PORTRAIT

TEXT BY
RON PILLING

FOREWORD BY
PARRIS N. GLENDENING, GOVERNOR

PHOTOGRAPHY BY
ROGER MILLER

USNA Color Parade

Roger Miller In His Union Square Studio

IMAGE PUBLISHING, LTD.
1411 Hollins Street / Union Square
Baltimore, MD 21223-2417
(TEL) 410-566-1222   (FAX) 410-233-1241
(E-MAIL) rmpl.ipl@verizon.net
(WEB PAGE) rogermillerphoto.com

DEDICATION

TO RACHEL

I would like to dedicate this book to my daughter. I can only hope that you are healthy, strong, happy and fair.

TO DAVE

I would like to dedicate this book to my brother . We are very different - and we are very much the same. I am just glad you have been there it has made a big difference in my life!

ROGER MILLER, 04-2000

SPECIAL THANKS

A very special thanks to **RUTH and CHARLES MILLER,** my parents, for their assistance, love, courage and belief in my work no matter what.

A very special thanks to **DAVID BOARMAN, JR.,** my associate, assistant photographer, advisor, critic, and friend for dealing with the pressures of doing this book. Unless you have lived through the excitement, hard work and frustration of doing a book, you have no idea!

A very special thanks to Governor **PARRIS N. GLENDENING** for doing the foreword to the book and for allowing me to do his portrait and the photos inside Government House.

A very special thanks to master **JIM HUMPHRIES** for his assistance, friendship and focus. I only wish we had more time to work out.

A very special thanks to **TOM CARTER** of Old Bay Financial for his assistance, friendship, advice and action.

A very special thanks to **SHERRY (LYNN) MOQUIN,** CPA for her financial advice, friendship and moral support over the years.

A very special thanks to all of the following who were of assistance in giving advice and comfort in doing the photos of all the **HISTORIC PROPERTIES OF ANNAPOLIS** to a sometimes confused photographer trying to capture all the beauty: **SANDRA ROSE** at Government House; **BARBARA HARWARD-TROSKA** at Government House; **JULIE CHRISTIAN** at Upton Scott House for allowing me to photograph her home and her friendly advice on how to contact the rest of historic Annapolis; **CARTER LIVELY** of Hammond Harwood House for his assistance with the photos and important advice on additional historic sites; **GREG STIVERSON** of London Town House & Gardens; **LYNN MANWARING** of the Historic Annapolis Foundation; **JUDI KARDASH** of Acton Hall; **FREDERICA STRUSE** of Ridout House; **GLENN CAMPBELL** of Historic Annapolis Foundation for his assistance; and **JANE McWILLIAMS** writer and historian for reviewing our historic text and her friendly advice.

ROGER MILLER, 04-2000

SPECIAL THANKS

A very special thanks to everyone at the **UNITED STATES NAVAL ACADEMY** for allowing me access to all their sites and activities during the last couple of years and especially all of the following for their assistance and always friendly advice: **JOHN R. RYAN,** Vice Admiral, U.S. Navy, Superintendent for allowing me to photograph Buchanan House; **KAREN MYERS,** Director of Media Relations for her always pleasant assistance in setting up most of my photo contacts at the Naval Academy and for proofing all our Naval Academy text; **DEBBIE BISHOP** for her always friendly help; **ENS, LISA SICKINGER** (who is now sailing the ocean blue) for my safe passage through the Naval maze; **LT. MATTHEW ARNOLD,** USNA Sailing Team for allowing me to sail with him; **JIM CHEEVERS,** Curator of the U.S. Naval Academy Museum for his modeling debut for this book and for checking the historic accuracy of all the Naval Academy text.

A very special thanks to everyone who assisted us in doing **PHOTOS OF SAILING** and boats in Annapolis especially the following: **BRUCE FARR , RUSSELL BOWLER** and **AMY FAZEKAS** of Farr Yacht Design, Ltd. for allowing us to do photos in their offices; **ANDREA GWINN** and **SCOTT MORRISON** of Sail Yard Inc. for some wondrous evenings of sailing and not caring if I used Scott's boat as a tripod; **BRIAN DALGLIESH** of Avon Marine for his wild ride chasing sailboats in the sun and **GARY JOBSON,** ESPN sailing commentator and a world class sailor of Annapolis for allowing me to do photos of him and his sailboat.

A very special thanks to everyone in the **MARYLAND STATE GOVERNMENT** who was of assistance in doing the book especially the following: **JIM LOUKAS, WALTER STILLWELL, ANN WALLACE** and **SUSAN CASEY** of the Governor's Office; **DR. EDWARD C. PAPENFUSE** and **MIMI CALVER** of the Maryland State Archives.

ROGER MILLER, 04-2000

CREDITS

Photography by ROGER MILLER
Design by DAVID MILLER and ROGER MILLER
Foreword by GOVERNOR PARRIS GLENDENING
Writing by RON PILLING
Editing by DAVE BOARMAN and ROGER MILLER

INFORMATION

SECOND EDITION, FIRST PRINTING 2000, SECOND PRINTING 2001
Library of Congress Control Number: 00-130101
ISBN # 0-911897-47-X
Printed in Hong Kong, China.

ORDERS

For direct orders please call or write for the specific pricing and the postage and handling to **IMAGE PUBLISHING, LTD**. at the above address. Discounts are available for stores, institutions and corporations, with minimum order requirements. You may also contact us for sales directly on our web page. The suggested retail price at the time of publication is **US$39.95.**

Construction began on the **Maryland State House** in 1772. This was the third State House building on this site and its large wooden dome still dominates both State Circle and the town of Annapolis. The current structure was expanded and improved in 1858, 1886 and 1902.

Please Note: All the photographs featured in this book are available as limited edition art prints.

With full sails, entrants in the traditional Wednesday evening races enter the Annapolis harbor from the Chesapeake Bay. The huge dome of the United States Naval Academy Chapel has a commanding harbor view on the right, with the State House dome and the steeple of St. Mary's Church looking over the water from across town.

TABLE OF CONTENTS

Governor Parris N. Glendening stands at the staircase in the entrance hall of Government House. Throughout his two terms in office, the Governor has hosted dignitaries, elected officials and citizens of all ages at the official residence. Schoolchildren and adults tour Government House to learn about Maryland's history.

FOREWORD
BY GOVERNOR PARRIS N. GLENDENING

Beautiful townhouses from centuries past... The pride and honor of America's Naval Academy... The oldest working State House in the nation... Booming businesses from Main Street shops to high-tech companies on the cutting edge of the knowledge-based economy. Annapolis, Maryland's state capital, uniquely blends the rich history of our past with the boundless hope of our future.

Photographer Roger Miller's latest journey into Maryland's past and present tells the definitive story of Annapolis as it stands today. You will begin Roger's tour with a visit to Maryland's State House, perhaps the greatest monument to our State's important role in American history. Completed in 1779, Maryland's State House was the nation's capital from November 1783 to August 1784, when the Continental Congress was housed in the building. Strolling through the State House you can stop by the Old Senate Chamber. Here, George Washington resigned his commission as commander-in-chief of the Continental Army in December 1783, and, a month later, the Treaty of Paris was ratified, officially ending the Revolutionary War.

Like Annapolis itself, the State House is more than a beautiful landmark of the past - it continues to shape the future. In the oldest working State House in America, legislators still meet as they did hundreds of years ago, but today they debate modern public policy and enact laws that improve the lives of 21st-century Marylanders.

As you travel around our majestic state capital with Roger, you will repeatedly see a city that is known throughout the world for its historic preservation, but is in fact quite modern. Just around the corner from the State House, while you explore the historic district's brick-lined streets and townhouses, you are steps away from companies with Internet connections to the world. You can stroll down to the waterfront that was once a thriving commercial port, and see why Annapolis is known today as the sailing capital of the world. You can observe a city that showcases its vibrant culture in buildings such as the Maryland Hall for Creative Arts. And you can witness a day in the life of a Naval Academy Midshipman and watch him or her follow the traditions of the past in order to become a leader in tomorrow's armed forces.

Through the lens of his camera, Roger Miller has captured the essence of Annapolis and the spirit of Maryland - charming, thriving, historic and contemporary. As you enjoy Roger's tour around the state capital, I invite you to come to Annapolis and experience its beauty and excitement for yourself. As our two million annual visitors can attest, Annapolis extends a warm welcoming hand to its guests and encourages them to return many times.

Parris N. Glendening

The sun sets over Spa Creek looking across the city dock and up Main Street to St. Anne's Church. To the right, the State House dominates the skyline from atop State Circle. This is the evening view which has welcomed sailors for centuries.

INTRODUCTION

When Royal Governor Francis Nicholson stepped from the deck of what was probably a small, locally-built wooden sailing craft onto the harbor quay of Anne Arundel Town, he came with a particular political purpose: to coronate the village at the confluence of the Severn River and Spa Creek as the capital of the English colony of Maryland. He had been petitioning the government in the colony's first capital, St. Mary's City, to remove the seat of government to Anne Arundel Town. In 1695, though the colony was scarcely sixty years old, Nicholson wished to found the colony on ground more centrally located in the province – geographically as well as politically. Shortly after his arrival he renamed the town Annapolis, in honor of Princess Anne, who later became the Queen of England.

Nicholson was thus the first in a line of thousands who came to Annapolis, left their important marks, and departed. He himself went on to be the Royal Governor of Virginia, Nova Scotia and finally South Carolina. "Native Son," a particularly American term, has little application in Annapolis, for her fame has largely been the product of visitors. Three centuries later little has changed - Annapolis hosts thousands of guests each year, many who come to achieve a measure of prominence for themselves and then go elsewhere to apply it. The town benefits always by their presence, and sometimes by their departure, too.

In every case, the nearness of the Chesapeake Bay has had something to do with the magnetic force that attracts people here. When Nicholson arrived, it was simply easier to get here by water. What would become U.S. Route 1 was but a dirt track through what was still inhospitable country. By the early 18th–century, Annapolis was already a growing port for the export of tobacco and the import of all manner of goods which under the shackle of English law could not be manufactured in the colonies.

To break those shackles, Marylanders who had already begun to think of themselves as "Americans" rather than as Englishmen came to Annapolis to join the incipient American Revolution. At the cessation of the war they returned to their plantations, to come again when it became necessary to lay the constitutional foundation for the new nation. Then, once again, most of them started homeward. Our most revered patriots - Washington, Jefferson, Madison and dozens of others - were part of the throng. General Lafayette received the adulation of the state when he came to Annapolis in 1824, then he returned to France.

So Annapolis learned early that she had better be hospitable when guests arrive, a lesson that has carried her through Revolution, Civil War, and the annual campaigns fought in the State House over one proposal or another when the Maryland Legislature is in session. The feet of tourists have worn away the threshold at Middleton's Tavern and other Annapolis inns, stirred the dust of narrow streets named for visitors (or those who never actually lived here) – Duke of Gloucester Street, Francis Street, Bladen Street and others. Government buildings bear the names of those from elsewhere, and halls on the campus of the United States Naval Academy are named for Americans who made their marks in spots on the globe as far away as Tripoli, Pearl Harbor, the Midway Islands, and Mobile Bay.

We come for the same reasons as the new millennium dawns. Sometimes the first glimpse of Annapolis is still from harborside, only from fiberglass sloops and throaty power yachts rather than ironclads and wooden-walled frigates. For many, it's still easier to get to Annapolis by water than by land, as is testified by the home ports neatly lettered on the transoms of visiting pleasure craft. Sailors find the same warm welcome in twenty-first century hostelries as they did in the taverns and inns of three hundred years past. They fill their galleys with groceries and their gas tanks with fuel; they do their laundry and re-stock their lockers; they make minor repairs in the rigging or stay for complete refittings; then they sail off for another port.

Each year a thousand-plus young Americans arrive in Annapolis for a longer visit: a stint as students at the Naval Academy. After they have tossed their hats in the air in celebration of their graduation and commissioning four years later they too will leave the waterfront town for points beyond. Some return to teach or in retirement, but for most their years in Annapolis, while perhaps their most formative, are very short. Others come to study at St. John's College. When the century-old ivy was cleared from the facade of McDowell Hall a few years ago, the autographs of countless students who had carved their names into the soft sandstone foundation were revealed - students who had come from country beyond the Annapolis city limits and who left to apply their hard-earned knowledge elsewhere as well.

Not long after Annapolis has rolled up the red carpet for the incoming freshmen, the annual pilgrimage of Senators and Delegates descends on Annapolis. Government House, the home of Maryland's governors, has been occupied by former Mayors of Baltimore, native-born Virginians and Delawareans. Only twice in 225 years has the mantle of Governor been worn by someone who called Annapolis home. Many went back to their local constituencies upon the conclusion of their administrations and many used their brief time in Annapolis to bootstrap their way to higher office in Washington.

If Annapolis were a town filled with only visitors, however, there would never have been an impetus to restore its fine old buildings and to respect its centuries of history. Some people do indeed call the place home - permanently. One person in particular was St. Clair Wright, an Annapolis woman with vision and backbone who, with a cadre of other loyal residents, founded Historic Annapolis, Inc. (now the Historic Annapolis Foundation) in 1952. Because of their efforts, the gas station that sat on City Dock is now gone, as well as the spider webs of utility lines that laced the old streets. Nearly 500 homes have been saved because of the determination of native Annapolitans.

Most everyone who comes and goes, or who comes and stays, is better in mind and body for having spent time in the state capital. Long after Supreme Court Justice Roger B. Taney completed his law studies in Annapolis he recalled the town as the "Athens of America." An early visitor called it the "Bath of America," noting its genteel manners, academia and fine hospitality. In 1896, a newspaper article complimented Annapolis as the "Venice of America."

Modern journalists seldom use the cliched "-of America," but as visitors depart Annapolis today the idea is still the same as it was for visitors decades ago. Their appetites for oysters and crabs from the Chesapeake have been sated. Their trunks are filled with goods from around the world. If only briefly, boaters regained their land legs. Legislators have garnered a roadway or a courthouse for their local communities. Everyone has a smile on their face for having spent time in Annapolis as they head for home, whether home is on Duke of Gloucester Street, doors from the State House, on the deck of an aircraft carrier, or in some distant part of the world.

Aerial View Looking East Towards Spa Creek and the Severn River

Annapolis has been the capital of Maryland since colonial days, and the State House has occupied high ground on State Circle since its construction. Narrow streets radiate from the circle in all directions, linking the seat of government to Government House (the governor's residence, in the right foreground) and to the rest of Annapolis.

HISTORIC ANNAPOLIS

On a cold afternoon in mid-January, a coterie of well-dressed Marylanders gather under the huge Tiffany stained-glass skylight in the Legislative Caucus Room, on Annapolis' State Circle. The talk is punctuated with 10-digit numbers, preceded by dollar signs. Ideas that will affect every citizen of the Old Line State, and will spread to all the other forty-nine as well, are hatched within these walls. The Maryland Legislature is holding session in the state capital, Annapolis, as it has done for over 300 years.

Once again, this tiny town, with its ancient narrow streets and centuries-old traditions, takes on an importance which its diminutive size would belie. Annapolis is still a leading American capital, true to its rich history.

The first session occurred shortly after colonial Governor Francis Nicholson moved the capital from St. Mary's City in 1695. He found in "Anne Arundel Town," as it was then known, an already-thriving town huddled around a harbor perfectly suited for the export of tobacco, the "vile weed" which was the backbone of the colony's economy. Nicholson had political reasons for making the move. The "Glorious Revolution" of 1688 had brought Protestant King William to the English throne, and Annapolis was the only Protestant bastion in Maryland. Nicholson was anxious to gain as much support in London as possible.

He wasted no time in turning the modest town into an appropriate capital. Annapolis was to be dominated by two stately circles. The nearest to the harbor, State Circle, was to have the seat of state power at its center. The construction of Maryland's first State House began immediately and was finished in 1697. Until then, the assembly met in a courthouse, built by one Major Dorsey, which stood near State Circle. Just to the west, early planners laid out Church Circle as a home to the Church of England.

Society followed suit. Annapolis gentlemen wore the latest fineries from England, brought in the same bottoms which hauled their tobacco to the mother country. Annapolis' "Golden Age" flourished from the mid-1700's until the Revolution. Fortunes were won and lost on the race track just outside the city on what is now West Street. The "Tuesday Club" mimicked other clubs in other cities, where well-heeled entrepreneurs gathered to eat and drink too much, write little plays about one another, and call each other clever nicknames. Other clubs were formed and one, the South River Club, still meets regularly.

Yet in spite of their close ties - intellectual, economic and otherwise - to London, Annapolitans enthusiastically supported the American Revolution. The passage of the Stamp Act in 1765 stirred the first patriotic tempers in Annapolis. While Sons of Liberty in other cities were burning tax collectors in effigy, a mob in Annapolis ran collector Zachariah Hood out of town. On October 15, 1774, the brigantine *Peggy Stewart* dropped anchor in the harbor with a load of hated, and highly-taxed, English tea. A gallows was built in front of shipowner Anthony Stewart's house as a hint of public sentiment. Stewart himself sailed the doomed boat a bit further upriver, and torched it. Annapolis had its own tea party.

There were no large battles on Maryland soil during the Revolution, though many troops passed through Annapolis. Among the most prominent wartime visitors was General Lafayette, who bivouacked here on his way to Yorktown in 1781. Lafayette was wined and dined in the town's finest homes, many of which had as brilliantly hosted English General Braddock twenty-five years earlier on his way to ignominious defeat at the hands of the French and native Americans.

After the conclusion of the Revolution, Congress met briefly in the State House, and an event which was as important a precedent as any other in American history took place on December 23, 1783. When General George Washington arrived at the State House that day, he commanded such respect that he could have declared himself King. Indeed, many among the young nation's leaders thought that a hereditary monarchy was the only way to rule a land of "rogues and brigands." Washington came not for coronation, however, but to resign his commission and step, at least temporarily, into private life. This demonstration of his faith in popular democracy set the stage for a government "of the people, by the people, and for the people." Just weeks later, Congress gathered in Annapolis to ratify the Treaty of Paris, which formally ended the Revolution.

Almost three years passed and Annapolis returned to the national limelight. Alexander Hamilton of New York, and Virginian James Madison, among other leaders, met here to map out our national political future. They recognized that the Articles of Confederation, which weakly bound the states together, were inadequate to the task of national governance. The Annapolis Convention adjourned in September, 1786, having called for another gathering in Philadelphia, from which our Constitution would be born.

Thus ended the early years Annapolis spent on the national stage. By the 1790's a visitor called it "a finished city." It was still the state capital, only without its pre-revolutionary extravagance. The Revolution permanently severed the ties to London and halted the flow of luxuries. Upstart Baltimore, whose port proved to be more efficient than Annapolis' because of its location further inland on the Patapsco River, eclipsed the old town economically.

None could deny the waterfront location, however, and for that reason the United States Naval Academy was relocated here in 1845, stemming a 50-year decline. Except for a brief period during the Civil War, the Naval Academy and Annapolis have been virtually synonymous terms. Nothing since has spurred such growth. The need for hotel rooms, taverns and restaurants resulted in a boom in the hospitality trade in a town still vaguely recalled for its colonial hospitality. Navy frigates, including the USS *Constitution* were stationed here for midshipman training. A host of small sailboats scudded across the harbor daily as crews learned port from starboard and sheet from halyard.

Annapolis plodded through the Victorian years and early 20th-century, hosting dignitaries including Lord Mountbatten, Mark Twain and Woodrow Wilson who came to the Naval Academy. Old patriotic fervor bubbled whenever sailors were sent overseas - to the Spanish-American War in 1898, and then to die in successive World Wars. The fine old mansions moldered, but at least remained on their foundations.

Little changed until the 1950's. A rumored visit in the 1920's to Annapolis by John D. Rockefeller, who was ostensibly in search of a colonial town to "restore" (he later, of course, chose Williamsburg), may have sparked local recognition of the architectural and historical treasure that was Annapolis. In 1952, Historic Annapolis, Inc. was founded to preserve what remained. The group saved the important William Paca House from demolition in 1965 and has, since its inception, served as the city's architectural watchdog and purveyor of history and tours. The result is one of the most pristinely-restored early cities in America.

Yet over the centuries one aspect of Annapolis life has never changed: the annual pilgrimage of lawmakers to the banks of the Severn River. Their chambers have grown, and they have commodious leather chairs on which to rest their legislative posteriors rather than the plain wooden Windsor chairs of two centuries earlier. But the issues are probably the same - taxes, road construction, schools, fisheries. It's a pretty sure bet that the State Senate and House of 1810 would recognize much of what goes on from January until April every year. It's business in Annapolis, as usual.

The Maryland State House - Cherry blossoms herald the coming of another Annapolis spring as well as the departure of the Maryland Legislature. From January to April of every year the State House is alive with debate as lawmakers consider Maryland's pressing issues. The domed capitol building has hosted state leaders for more than two centuries.

State House - The last of a series of four expansions in 1902 brought the State House to its current size. Atop is the largest wooden dome in America, seen here from the western facade with cherry blossoms in early spring. The cherry blossoms in Annapolis symbolize not only the changing of seasons, but of the whole tempo of the city. Legislators leave town for home and the "serious" business of sailing and enjoying life on the bay takes over.

Hanging in the **State House dome** is a replica of the Shaw Flag, one of the many varieties of 13-star, 13-stripe flags that flew in the nation's earliest years. The Shaw Flag is not always displayed as the exhibits in the public areas of the State House are always changing. By the time the United States came into being, lawmakers had been visiting the stately brick building for over a decade. The interior of the original building has been immaculately preserved.

The State House has become a lasting symbol of Annapolis and Maryland. Whether on a snow covered night or a sunny spring morning, the sight of the State House dome reaching above State Circle is a comforting landmark. The present wooden dome was designed and built in 1785 to 1788 by architect Joseph Clark.

Roger B. Taney Statue

Dome of the State House

State House - Roger B. Taney was the Chief Justice of the Supreme Court from 1836 until his death in 1864. Born in nearby Calvert County, Taney previously served in Annapolis as a State Senator. Of his many decisions, none was more far-reaching than the 1857 *Dred Scott vs. Sandiford*, in which Taney declared that slaves had no right to sue in Federal court and that Congress had no power to exclude slavery from the territories. The decision, based on current Constitutional law, set the stage for the coming Civil War. Taney is remembered today with a monument on the State House lawn.

Senate Chamber

House of Delegates Chamber

Old Treasury Building

State House - Contemporary Senators spend three months of every year in comfortable leather armchairs in the new (1902) Senate Chamber (left). Maryland has a bicameral legislature, and members of the House of Delegates have their own chamber (top right) in the State House. On the grounds, the little brick Treasury Building, built in 1735-37 by Patrick Creaph, stands in the shadows of the capital building. It now serves as the tour office for Historic Annapolis.

Maryland's **Original Senate Chamber** was the setting of the ratification of the Treaty of Paris on January 14, 1784, which ended the American Revolution. In the weeks prior, George Washington had returned to this chamber to resign his commission, an event which as much as any other determined the democratic course of American government.

Maryland's State House is the oldest still in use in the country. Construction on the original State House was begun in 1772 and it was placed in use in 1779. From November 26, 1783 to August 19, 1784 it served as the capital of the newly formed United States. During that time the State House was home to the Continental Congress and there was much talk and rumor that Annapolis would become the nation's permanent capital.

Snow Covered Grounds of Government House

Government House - Since the end of the Revolutionary War, Maryland has provided a home for its governors and their families. The first official governor's residence was called Jennings House and was located on a large plot of land that sloped gracefully to the Severn River. The house and its grounds were sold to the U.S. Naval Academy in 1866 and a new Government House was built on State Circle across the street from the State House.

Government House With Gardens in Spring Bloom

Government House, since its construction in 1870 as a high-Victorian mansion with a Mansard roof and large porches, has undergone a complete identity change. The five-part Georgian country house we see today was the result of a major renovation that took place during the administration of Governor Harry Whinna Nice in 1935-36. It was felt at the time that a Georgian-style residence would be more in keeping with the colonial character of Annapolis.

21

The staff people at **Government House** keep it humming as a center of the political and social life of Annapolis. Government House hosts exhibitions of art from Maryland's fine art museums, private collections and the Maryland State Archives. A large portrait of Queen Henrietta Maria (top right), wife of King Charles I of England and in whose honor Maryland was named, is featured in the entrance hall.

Within **Government House**, there are seven public rooms: the entrance hall, the library, the reception room, the parlor, the conservatory, the drawing room and the state dining room. These rooms are filled with antique and reproduction furnishings associated with different periods in Maryland's history. The large drawing room (bottom right) with its grand piano is a perfect setting for musical concerts and other entertainment.

Front of Paca House On Prince George Street

William Paca House - William Paca, one of Maryland's signatories to the Declaration of Independence, began building his stately brick home in 1763 after marrying a wealthy heiress. He sold the house in 1780, served as Maryland's governor from 1782 to 1785, and later built an even more sumptuous home on Maryland's Eastern Shore.

Dining Room

Rear Stair Hallway

William Paca House - Later years found the Paca House engulfed by the massive Carvel Hall Hotel, and its rescue was the crowning achievement of Historic Annapolis Foundation. Careful examination of over 20 layers of paint and wallpaper enabled Historic Annapolis to reproduce the original colors chosen by Paca when it restored this small dining room and gracious staircase.

William Paca House - Paca's intricate plasterwork did not survive the depredations of the Carvel Hall Hotel, but remaining evidence allowed its recreation in the Prussian blue dining room. The rear terrace affords visitors a commanding view of Paca's extensive gardens. The hotel was built squarely atop the garden, and its demolition in 1965 cleared the way for the recreation of the Pacas' landscape. Extensive archaeological excavations, 18th-century garden design books and background details in a portrait of Paca by Annapolis artist Charles Willson Peale provided the clues needed to bring the garden back to life.

The Paca Gardens Looking South

The restored **William Paca Garden** is a wonderful example of urban garden design at the close of the colonial period. It features formal boxwood, a lovely Chinese Chippendale bridge, as well as more functional herb and kitchen plantings.

Interior of St. Anne's Church

St. Anne's Church - Dark wooden beams and distinctive woodwork mark the interior of St. Anne's Church as the Romanesque Revival style. Its stone altar and font were carved by Maryland's most famous sculptor, William Henry Rinehart. The walnut pews, pulpit and lectern date from 1859.

St. Anne's Church - Church Circle

St. Anne's Church - This is the third church to serve parishioners on this site since St. Anne's was established in 1692 as one of thirty Church of England parishes in the colony. During the Revolution, most members refused to attend a church headed by the King of England, and they deserted it again in 1861 because church leaders, contrary to local sentiment, sided with the Union.

The Drawing Room

Northeast Bedchamber

The Best Bedchamber

Dining Room

Hammond-Harwood House exemplifies the very best of British North America's architecture. Constructed in 1774 by wealthy planter Matthias Hammond, the house typifies the fashionable Palladian villa style favored by Annapolis' colonial elite. Built to plans by one of America's first true architects, Oxford born, London trained, William Buckland, the house would eventually be owned by Buckland's descendants the Harwood family. There is little question why this colonial masterpiece is acclaimed the "Jewel of Annapolis!"

Garden Facade

Maryland Avenue Facade

Hammond-Harwood House features what is considered "colonial America's most beautiful doorway." Ornate carved decorations by English craftsmen embellish this perfect classical entrance which beckons to the treasures within. The garden facade gracefully dominates the peaceful green area devoted to ancient boxwood and serene contemplation. Created by noted colonial revival landscape architect Alden Hopkins, this enclosure provides a haven for visitors from the hubbub of busy modern Annapolis.

31

Front on Maryland Avenue

Staircase In Entrance Hall

Detail of Ornate Plaster Work

Front Staircase

Chase-Lloyd House - A brash young lawyer named Samuel Chase began building his Annapolis home in 1769. Though his career eventually rewarded him as a signer of the Declaration of Independence, a chief judge and later as an associate Supreme court justice, Chase ran out of money during construction and was forced to sell the unfinished house. It was purchased by Colonel Edward Lloyd who hired the most sought after designer of Georgian homes, William Buckland, to complete his mansion. It is famous for Buckland's elaborate plaster cornices, trim work and ceilings and an ingenuous cantilevered stairway.

East Street Facade

Intricate Wood and Plaster Work

James Brice House - It is no coincidence that the James Brice House was chosen as a headquarters for the International Union of Bricklayers and Allied Craftsmen in 1982. The masonry is extraordinary on this five-part Georgian mansion, which took seven years beginning in 1767 to complete. With its massive chimneys, it rises sixty feet from the street.

Tobacco Prise House

The Barracks

The Barracks

The Barracks - General Lafayette passed through Annapolis on his way to victory at Yorktown in 1781. While he no doubt was hosted in the town's finest mansions, more modest houses similar to The Barracks were commandeered to house soldiers on their way to battle. The Barracks is a museum that interprets Maryland's role in the War for American Independence. **Tobacco Prise House** - Within view of the harbor, an early 19th-century warehouse and replica tobacco press or "prise" remind modern visitors of Annapolis' once-flourishing trade in "sot-weed."

Shiplap House - Pinkney Street was lined with some of the earliest businesses in Annapolis, and the Shiplap House stands as a reminder of Annapolis' early mercantile years. Built about 1715, it has served as a tavern, a store, a cabinetmaking shop, an artist's studio and a tenement. Its name is derived from its flush beaded, or "shiplap," wooden siding. Today, the building houses office and exhibit spaces of Historic Annapolis Foundation.

Liberty Tree

Randall Hall

Liberty Bell

St. John's College is the third oldest college in the United States, founded in 1696. It is respected among academicians worldwide because of its unique curriculum, based exclusively on the study of the great books of western civilization. Each of the 400 students follows the same course of study, reading works of history, philosophy, literature, mathematics and science. Commencement was traditionally held under the branches of Maryland's Liberty Tree, an ancient tulip poplar under which the Sons of Liberty met. Unfortunately, the tree had to be removed in 1999.

McDowell Hall At the Center of Campus

In 1742, Colonial Governor Thomas Bladen determined that he needed a grandiose mansion and work was begun on what is now **McDowell Hall**, on the campus of St. John's. But the Maryland General Assembly differed and refused to appropriate the money. The half-finished building sat for forty years until it was turned over to the College. Classes still meet here.

Peggy Stewart House

Sands House

Peggy Stewart House is noted for its rare "all-header bond" (the short edges of the bricks are visible from the facade), and as the focus of Annapolis' own Tea Party. Owner Anthony Stewart attempted to land a cargo of tea in Annapolis, and outraged citizens descended on his home in protest. Chastened, Stewart set fire to his own vessel.
The Sands House is believed to be the oldest surviving house in Annapolis, and was probably facing Prince George Street before 1700. It housed a tavern and was later occupied by a joiner, a merchant and a shipwright. John Sands, a mariner, bought it just before the Revolution and it has remained in the same family since.

Carroll House With St. Mary's Steeple To Right, St. Anne's To Left

Carroll House - Charles Carroll of Carrollton, who was born in this majestic house on the banks of Spa Creek, was the wealthiest man in America when he put his name to the Declaration of Independence. The Carrolls were Catholic (Cousin John was the first Catholic Bishop in the United States), and the public practice of their faith was forbidden in the years just before the Revolution. Not ones to give in, the Carrolls held private ceremonies in the Annapolis home.

Ogle Hall owes its name to the family of Governor Samuel Ogle, who lived here from 1747 until 1752. George Washington dined here on October 1, 1773 with Governor Ogle's son Benjamin, an event noted in Washington's diary. The 1739 house was embellished in the Georgian fashion between 1765 and 1774 and in the century and a half that followed a succession of prominent Annapolitans lived here. In 1945 it became the Alumni House for the United States Naval Academy. The comfortable home, furnished with antiques and reproductions, is the gathering place for distinguished visitors to the Yard.

Barrister House - Yet another Charles Carroll, this time the patriarch of the Anglican Carrolls, built this house in 1723 after amassing a fortune in the eight short years following his arrival in Annapolis. It is named for his more famous son, Charles Carroll the Barrister , who was a leading patriot in Revolutionary Maryland. In 1955, Historic Annapolis moved it to the campus of St. John's College from its original site on Main Street.

Upton Scott House is one of the earliest grand Georgian homes in Annapolis. Begun in 1762 and completed in 1764, the house was constructed by William Brown, builder and resident of nearby London Town. He built the house for Dr. Upton Scott and his wife, Elizabeth Ross. Francis Scott Key, the great nephew of Elizabeth Ross, lived in the house while attending St. John's College. It is rumored that he later composed the final draft of the "Star Spangled Banner" in his upstairs bedroom.

Dining Room

Living Room

Entrance Hallway

Chapel Bedroom

Upton Scott House, like many in Annapolis, holds its share of stories – some fact, some alleged. It is said that George Washington was a guest here, and many historians believe the house was part of the mid-nineteenth century Underground Railroad, citing the tunnels under the basement which lead to Spa Creek as evidence. In 1872 the residence was acquired by the School Sisters of Notre Dame, and for ninety-four years the property was used as a convent. The Upton Scott House became a private residence in 1968. The present owners, Paul and Julie Christian, are painstakingly restoring the home to its former grandeur.

Ridout House - This fine all-header bond brick house has been in the Ridout family since it was built by John Ridout shortly after his marriage in 1764. Ridout arrived in Annapolis as a young, Oxford-educated secretary to colonial Governor Horatio Sharpe. He chose Mary Ogle, the daughter of Governor Samuel Ogle, as his bride, thus cementing a position in Annapolis society that has lasted ever since.

Ridout House - Two days before Christmas, 1783, Mary Ridout walked from her home to the old Senate Chambers when George Washington came to resign his commission. Congress was then assembled in the State House, and both Senate and House Members, with entourages of ladies and hangers-on were in attendance. "The General seem'd so much affected himself that every body felt for him. He addressed Congress in a short speech...Many tears was shed," she wrote to her mother in England.

Acton Hall is demonstrably Georgian in design, a style that worshiped symmetry. The centered entrance is flanked by identical facades topped with massive, matching chimneys that parallel the front. The non-symmetrical wing on the right was added somewhere between 1866 and 1900. The original land grant, given to Richard Acton in 1658 for a plantation, was nearly as large as the entire original survey of Annapolis. The house itself was built by John Hammond before the Revolution.

Living Room

Dining Room

Back Facade and Garden

Acton Hall remained a working farm with large orchards well into the early 1900's . There is no question that there was an office both for the farm and the wharf. The wharf at the back of the house pre-dates city dock and is believed to be where the first ships docked in Annapolis. The house was purchased by James D. Murray, first paymaster of the Navy, in 1832. Captain Murray was instrumental in bringing the Naval Academy to Annapolis. By 1972 the property had fallen into a state of disrepair. Restoration efforts were undertaken by the Brown family in 1976 and completed by Jack Bridges in 1981.

Banneker-Douglass Museum - A congregation of free African Americans built Mount Moriah Church on Franklin Street in 1875 and parishioners worshiped here until January 1973. By November the building stood vacant and vandalized, stripped of its magnificent stained glass windows, until it was saved from demolition by the Maryland Commission on African American History and Culture. It was dedicated in 1984 as the Banneker-Douglass Museum and is the state's official repository for materials of African American heritage. Its collections of art, rare books, artifacts, photographs and historical archives preserves and shares Maryland's African American heritage.

The Annapolis Inn, an elegant Bed & Breakfast at 144 Prince George Street in the historic district of Annapolis, was built by Mr. Thomas Rutland circa 1770. Financial difficulties forced Mr. Rutland to sell his home within several months to Dr. James Murray, a prominent physician in Annapolis. Dr. Murray was physician to Thomas Jefferson during Jefferson's years in Annapolis and several of his sons-in-law were signers of the Declaration of Independence. In the cellar of the house, a tunnel of the Underground Railroad which led to the harbor can still be seen.

The William Brown House at Historic London Town and Gardens is where travelers between Philadelphia and Williamsburg often stopped before the Revolution. The surviving inn portrays tavern life in the eighteenth century, and the log tobacco barn adjoining the inn reminds us of the economic backbone of the Maryland colony.

The William Brown House at London Town is all that remains of what was once a thriving settlement on the banks of the South River just below Annapolis. The gracious 3-story inn, dating from 1760, is surrounded by eight acres of woodland gardens with wildflower trails and an extensive on-going archaeological investigation. London Town's success depended on the tobacco trade and the ferry crossing over the South River. Both gradually declined in importance and by the early 19th-century the town had largely disappeared.

Noon Formation is Completed as Battalions File Into Bancroft

Noon Formation brings the entire Brigade of Midshipmen onto Tecumseh Court fronting Bancroft Hall. With the exception of the winter months, Noon Formation occurs every day before the men and women are allowed to file into the dining room for the mid-day meal.

U.S. NAVAL ACADEMY

To develop midshipmen morally, mentally and physically and to imbue them with the highest ideals of duty, honor and loyalty in order to provide graduates who are dedicated to a career of naval service and have potential for future development in mind and character to assume the highest responsibilities of command, citizenship and government. The mission statement of the United States Naval Academy about says it all.

Each year more than a thousand plebes arrive in Annapolis to try to live up to the Academy's mission. They face a summer that is a cross between boot camp and fraternity initiation with a few of the less appealing aspects of monastic life thrown in. Forget the triumvirate most dear to undergraduates: cars, dates and beer. Students here have committed to a lot more than a simple bachelor's degree. Don't come here if you don't like sports and don't come here if your big goal in life is to be a doctor or a lawyer one midshipman advised. Nine years of military life is the minimum - four at the academy followed by five years as an officer in the U.S. Navy or Marine Corps. The commission is as prized as the academic degree.

For the new arrivals, and many who have preceded them, Annapolis is synonymous for the Yard, as the USNA is called among its inhabitants. The two have, since the inception of the Academy in 1845, been inseparable. The growth of Annapolis is inextricably linked to the Academy. Its restaurants cater to students, their families and Academy staff. Its hotels are filled with student families for Homecoming and Commissioning Week. Crisp white dress uniforms, worn proudly and with all the reverence one would expect, dot the narrow streets on the few weekends when midshipmen are granted liberty. Naval Academy boats fill the Annapolis harbor.

The genesis of the Academy was an ill-fated cruise aboard the U.S. Brig *Somers* in 1842. Aboard was a crew of teenaged naval apprentices who would ideally become career officers. Discipline deteriorated, however, and there was a determined attempt to commit a mutiny. Held accountable were a midshipman, Philip Spencer, and two enlisted personnel. The three swung from the yardarm. News of the mutiny shocked the nation, and steps were taken to expand the limited educational resources at the Naval Asylum in Philadelphia.

Secretary of the Navy George Bancroft took steps to transfer a defunct army installation called Fort Severn to the Navy. The Fort was at Windmill Point, adjacent to the Annapolis harbor, on land that had been bought from the Dulany family. On October 10, 1845, the Naval School officially opened with a class of fifty students and a seven-man faculty. In 1850 the school became the United States Naval Academy. A new curriculum included ordnance, navigation, naval tactics and gunnery, plus French, chemistry, English and history. Summers were to be spent in rigorous shipboard training. The modern course of study is certainly more sophisticated and technological, but no less demanding.

Midshipmen follow not only their grade point average, but also a regimented demerit system to regulate conduct. Demerits have no overall effect on academic averages, but they do play a large role in determining class standing. The pressure to excel, to succeed, to conform and to dedicate inculcates every aspect of life at the Yard. Try to imagine this philosophy in any other undergraduate school. Since the day the first midshipmen embarked at the West Street Station, seven generations of graduates have served heroically in eight wars. The student body has changed to reflect the evolution of American

society; the first female midshipmen were admitted in 1976. The campus itself has grown to accommodate the new demands on modern warfare and government. The original ten acres expanded to 338. The ragtag collection of wooden buildings that made up Fort Severn were gradually razed, the fort itself finally disappearing in 1909. Replacing the decrepit buildings are a collection of grand, gray brick and granite halls that say in their permanency as much about the gravity of their mission as the mission statement itself. While there is a variety of architecture, from French Renaissance to contemporary styles, the use of copper mansard roofs throughout tie the campus together.

Bancroft Hall, conceived in 1895 and begun in 1901 by New York architect Ernest Flagg, is the largest dormitory in the country, and the largest building at the Yard. It is home to the entire midshipman brigade of 4,000. The dining hall can accommodate all of them at once, chowing down on a thousand loaves of bread each morning and, on the occasion they are served, about 8000 donuts. There are four and a half miles of corridors.

The huge dormitory was the beginning of an expansion that created Dahlgren and MacDonough Halls in 1903 and a dozen other gray edifices since. On June 3, 1904, the cornerstone to the Chapel, the Cathedral of the Navy, was laid. The tallest building at the Academy, the Chapel's copper dome is visible from well out into the Chesapeake Bay. Inside are solemn reminders of why every midshipman is here: Admiral David Farragut's Civil War prayer book and Bible, and the crypt of John Paul Jones, the Father of the American Navy. Jones fought in the American Revolution and died in Paris in 1792. His remains stayed in the French capital for 113 years. On January 26, 1913, the flag-draped coffin was carried to the Chapel crypt. The crypt is the only part of the Chapel not designed by Flagg. It was created by another Beaux Art educated architect, Whitney Warren. An honor guard stands sentinel at all times when the crypt is open to visitors.

Every corner of the Yard has its memorial - a vast array of monuments and bronze tablets recalling either a building that once stood at the site or another place, often in a far-off land, where sailors and Marines fought and died. The Tripoli Monument immortalizes six naval officers who lost their lives fighting the Barbary Pirates in 1804, one of our earliest naval engagements. Captain Stephen Decatur captured the British frigate Macedonian in the War of 1812, and the figurehead of the captive, surrounded by four eighteen-pound guns of the period, stands near Maury Hall.

Preble Hall houses the Naval Academy Museum, whose artifacts describe the lives and sacrifices of graduates from the Revolution through Desert Storm. There are fragments from the most famous ships in our history as well as possessions of John Paul Jones, Stephen Decatur, Oliver Hazard Perry, David Farragut (Damn the Torpedoes...) and others. The museum is also home to the impressive Henry Huddleston Rogers Collection of exquisite ship models.

A quiet but stolid presence alongside the colonial streets of Annapolis, the United States Naval Academy has an effect that leaps its gray walls. Midshipmen have taken their memories of the tiny town to the beaches of Normandy, the hellish Murmansk Run, Cam Rahn Bay and the air over Baghdad. If they are lucky, many choose to retire to the town where they first donned the Navy blue. When Secretary Bancroft put his pen on the map at the mouth of the Severn in 1845 it was an auspicious moment for Annapolis, and another singular event in American history for the ancient capital.

Midshipmen Marching At Color Parade

Unlike most colleges and universities, the Naval Academy challenges its students with not only academic achievement but physical and military expertise as well. For their four years of training, the midshipmen will receive a commission as an officer in the Navy or Marine Corps along with their Bachelor of Science degree.

A YP Training Ship Maneuvers Just Off the Academy Grounds

Tiny Fort Severn, at the mouth of the river it was named for, was an Army base intended to protect Annapolis from enemy attack by water. Being outdated to this purpose, the War Department transferred the 10 acre plot of land to the Navy in August of 1845 as the site for a new naval institute of higher learning. The campus has since grown to 338 acres, known as "The Yard," and accommodates an enrollment of 4,000 midshipmen.

Marching in formation is still practiced at "The Yard." At one time midshipmen marched everywhere they went but that ended just over 30 years ago. Discipline is military-strict and uniforms are worn for every activity. The day begins with reveille and ends with lights out. Rooms in the nation's largest dormitory - Bancroft Hall - must be ready for white-glove inspection at all times.

Color Parade Formation In Front of Bancroft Hall

At the Naval Academy, the student body is the Brigade of Midshipmen. It is divided into six battalions, each of which is further divided into five companies. Formations like the one above exemplify the bond that grows between company members. "You make friendships that last forever. When everyone is going through the same challenges, you find that a very close-knit group develops."

Memorial Hall, inside Bancroft Hall, commemorates all alumni of the Naval Academy who have given their lives in battle for their country since the Academy was established in 1845. With its intricate parquet floors and monumental crystal chandeliers, the Hall is dwarfed only by the broad view it affords to the Chesapeake Bay. The credo "Don't Give Up The Ship" is sewn on the flag carried by Captain Oliver Hazard Perry into the Battle of Lake Erie, a decisive American victory in the War of 1812. The flag survived the battle, and flies today at one of the Academy's most hallowed monuments. Beneath it are the names of all Academy graduates who have died in active service.

Bancroft Hall - In 1899 architect Ernest Flagg was commissioned to rebuild the Academy, and Bancroft Hall was one of his first projects. Flagg's training at the Ecole des Beaux Arts in Paris is obvious in the edifices he created, architecturally combining the finest design elements of the late nineteenth century to reflect the glorious mission of the Academy. Flagg originally intended to use red brick for the new Academy, but a powerful granite lobby in Congress urged the use of Maine granite.

The Rotunda lies beneath Bancroft's towering dome. Only upon completion of the rigorous and demanding four-year curriculum are midshipmen allowed to enter the Rotunda through the center front door. The hall is named after George Bancroft, who as Secretary of the Navy founded the Academy in 1845.

The Rotunda of Bancroft Hall

Bancroft Hall - The Beaux Arts tradition in architecture, of which Bancroft Hall's designer Ernest Flagg was a disciple, returned to classical Greece and Rome for much of its inspiration. "The rites of daily life are ritualized by suitable rooms - le decor de la vie," according to Flagg's contemporary, architect John Barrington Bayley. "They must be classical rooms because classical architecture is the only architecture that expresses human dignity and greatness."

Tiffany Windows

Interior of Chapel

Pipe Organ - Naval Academy Chapel

Aerial Shows Chapel's Shape of a Cross

U.S. Naval Academy Chapel - Stained glass windows, many from the famed Tiffany Studios in New York, in the apse and transepts of the Naval Academy Chapel commemorate Naval heroes of the past - Porter, Farragut and Sampson. A monumental pipe organ with over five thousand pipes reigns on either side of the altar on these hallowed grounds. Each May, many newly-commissioned Ensigns (Navy) and Second Lieutenants (Marine Corps) march directly from graduation to dignified weddings in this sublime sanctuary. The floor plan of the Chapel is in the shape of a Latin cross, with a towering, copper-covered dome.

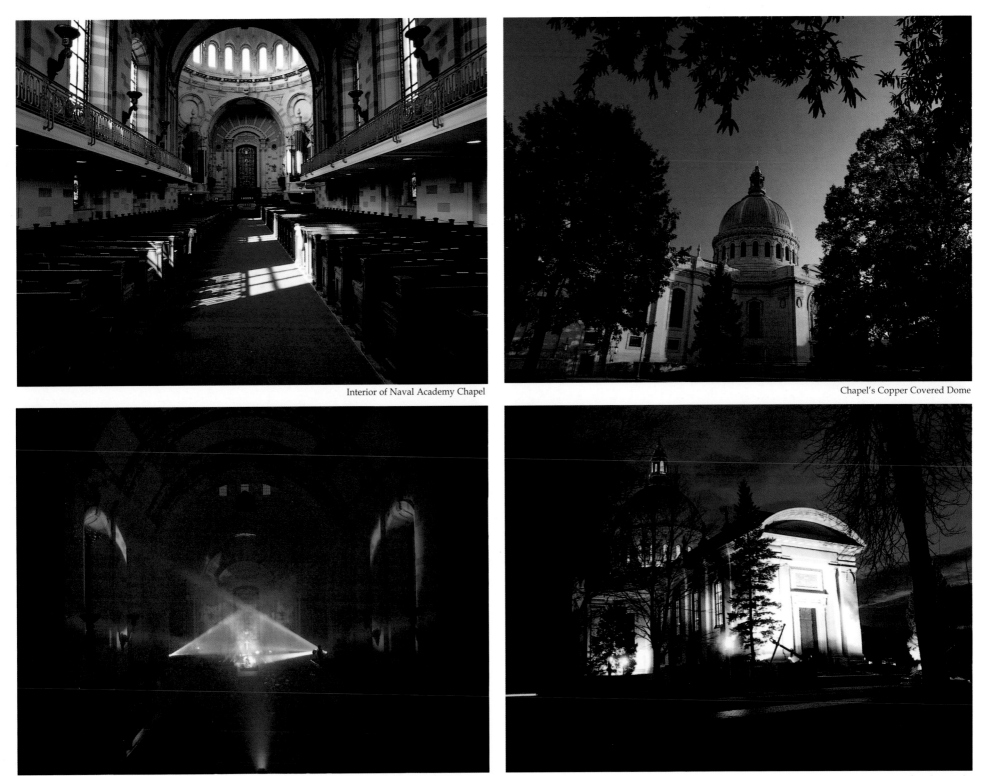

Interior of Naval Academy Chapel

Chapel's Copper Covered Dome

Halloween Performance

Chapel At Night

The cornerstone of the **Naval Academy Chapel**, the "Cathedral of the Navy," was laid in 1904. Destined to be the "architectural crown" of the Academy, Flagg poured his soul into its design and decoration. Every square inch is of some reverent significance to members of the Brigade, past and present. The monumental bronze doors - ten feet wide and twenty-four feet tall - were created by a young American sculptor, Evelyn Beatrice Longman. The Academy shows a lighter side each October when the Naval Academy Chapel plays host to the now annual Halloween performance, complete with organist and laser-light show.

Dome of the Naval Academy Chapel

Bronze Eagle in the Chapel

A tall bronze eagle stands proudly near the altar of the **Naval Academy Chapel**, while the dome depicts the night sky as it has been seen by countless Academy graduates from the rolling decks of wooden-walled frigates and steel battleships.

Naval Academy Chapel Crypt - The remains of America's first great Naval hero, John Paul Jones, lie in the most hallowed part of this sacred hall. Jones began his career in America when he volunteered his services to the Continental Congress in1775. He won every engagement into which he led forces, including the only two decisive American victories in the Revolution - one being the capture of the British HMS *Serapis* from his ship the *Bonhomme Richard*. When his flag was carried away and his surrender was demanded, Jones replied "I have not yet begun to fight." In 1790 Jones settled in Paris, where he died at the age of 45 in 1792. The marble sarcophagus, supported by four bronze dolphins, was given as a gift by the people of France.

Tecumseh

Tripoli Monument

Detail of Bancroft Hall

The warrior Tecumseh has come to symbolize everything for which Academy graduates strive. The original wooden figurehead of the 1836 USS Delaware, which is displayed in the Visitor's Center, was carved to represent Tamanend, Chief of the Delawares. It was nicknamed "Tecumseh" by the midshipmen in the late 1890's. The bronze copy has been in the Naval Academy Yard since 1930. The campus is dotted with memorials, including the Tripoli Monument. On September 4, 1804, six Naval officers were killed in the Battle of Tripoli, one of the fledgling Navy's first engagements. The monument, carved in Italy only two years after the loss, commemorates the courage of these early American seamen.

Macedonian Monument

Tecumseh With War Paint

Mexican War Monument

Captain Stephen Decatur captured the British frigate Macedonian in the War of 1812, and the figurehead of the captive, surrounded by four eighteen-pound guns of the period, stands near Maury Hall. Another quartet of guns, this time Spanish twelve-pounders, guard the Mexican War Monument. Erected in 1848, it was the first monument created especially for The Yard. Engraved around the base are the names of four midshipmen who fought and died in the Mexican War. The Tecumseh figure was renamed by midshipmen to honor the Shawnee warrior chief. He is decorated with war paint for all home football games, Commissioning Week and Alumni Weekend.

Buchanan House - An inventory of Naval Academy buildings in 1895 found many to be in terrible disrepair, too costly to renovate. A massive building program was instituted that produced the campus as it is recognized today. Originally, the Superintendent's quarters were to be in a newly-restored Maryland Governor's Mansion, but architect Ernest Flagg instead designed and built Buchanan House, which has been home to Academy Superintendents since 1909.

Dining Room

Front Parlor

Sun Porch

Entrance Hallway

Buchanan House, with over sixteen thousand square feet and thirty-four rooms, has entertained kings and prime ministers, admirals and Presidents. The home is comfortably furnished with antiques and reproductions, including a pair of corner cabinets which belonged to Academy founder George Bancroft. There is a marble-topped table which was used aboard the USS *Constitution*, "Old Ironsides." A dessert table in the dining room belonged to Commodore Thomas Truxtun, who served on American privateers during the Revolution.

The Naval Academy Museum houses one of the finest collection of ship models in the world, each constructed within a few years of the type of ship it represents. Most were bequeathed to the Academy by Colonel Henry Huddleston Rogers in 1935. Rogers collected over one hundred models, many more than 250 years old. The pride of the collection are the models carved of bone by French prisoners of war during the Napoleonic wars of 1802-1815.

Dahlgren Hall was built in 1903 as the Academy armory, but was converted into a student recreation facility in 1974. The conversion won two awards from the American Institute of Architects for completely changing the function of the building without altering its fabric or architectural design. Dahlgren is generously hung with items associated with American naval history. Visitors find the bow and stern ornaments of Admiral Dewey's flagship the USS *Olympia*, from which he defeated the Spanish at Manilla Bay in 1898. A Navy N3N3 double-winged float plane, nicknamed "yellow peril," hangs from the ceiling.

Each of the thirty companies of midshipmen participates in the annual "Color Company" competition. Military bearing and "spit-n-polish" are an important part of the contest, in which companies vie for points for academic, athletic and professional achievement. The company that lands on top is recognized during Commissioning Week and enjoys special privileges during the coming academic year.

Midshipmen Hats hang Outside a Classroom

There is a very serious academic side to Academy life which is invisible to most visitors. Midshipmen are here for an education, and a curriculum unique to the demands of the Navy greets incoming freshmen (or Plebes, in Academy jargon). There is a heavy grounding in physical and natural sciences and engineering - so much that every graduate receives a Bachelor of Science degree. Midshipmen may choose an academic major directed toward developing their individual interests from scientific and military fields as well as from the humanities and social sciences.

Plebe Summer

I-Day

I-Day

First Of Many Haircuts

When new arrivals walk through the gates of The Yard just weeks after completing high school they are in for a summer that will test their mettle and almost overnight turn them from adolescents into Midshipmen. Induction Day, or I-Day as it is known, is the beginning of "Plebe Summer" (the term is taken from the Latin "Plebian," the lowest class of Roman society). It is filled with sixteen-hour days that begin at dawn with rigorous exercise and end in complete exhaustion.

Workouts Are Well Under Way By Sunrise

By September, Plebes are in top physical condition. Mental acuity is sharpened - Plebes learn to think on their feet, to react quickly under stress. In one of the Academy's fleet of small sailboats, Plebes learn to respect the power of nature, and aboard one if its motorboats they learn basic navigation and seamanship. When the Brigade returns to Annapolis from summer training, Plebes are ready for the challenges that await them as the academic year opens.

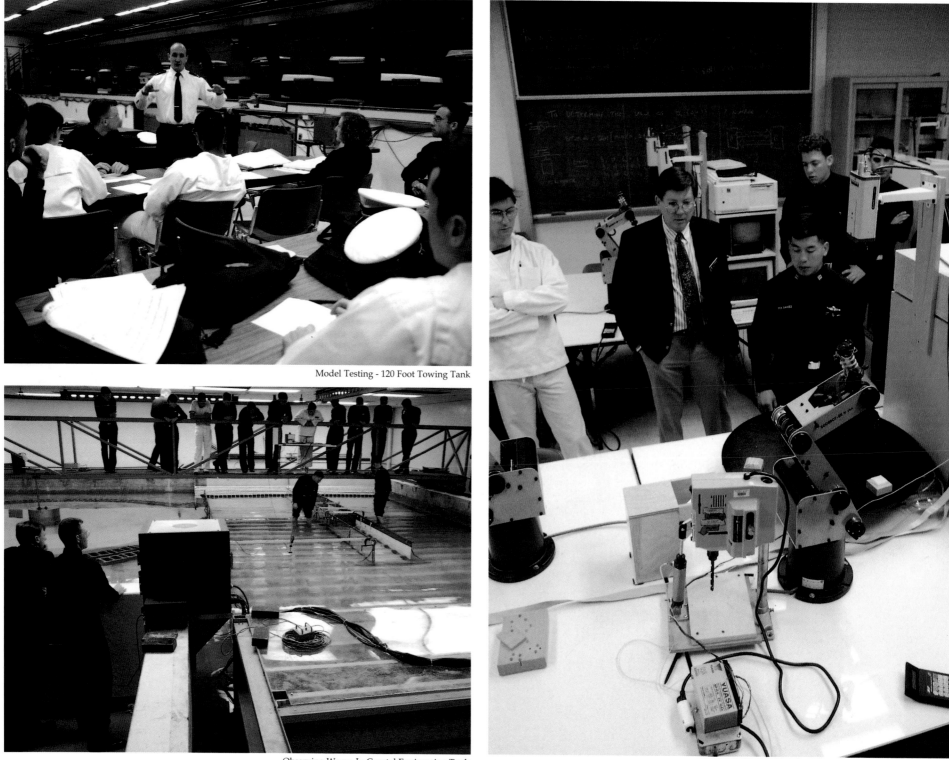

Model Testing - 120 Foot Towing Tank

Observing Waves In Coastal Engineering Tank

Robotics Training Lab

Naval Academy classes are small, ranging from ten to twenty-two students. Laboratories are taught by the same professors who conduct the lecture sessions, an important part of a curriculum so heavy in technical fields.

Lab Studies Propeller Design and Performance

Facilities are all state-of-the-arts, with a jet propulsion lab, wind tunnels, a nuclear reactor, and a satellite earth station on campus in addition to more conventional laboratory facilities. Here a group of Midshipmen study cavitation waves produced by propeller action.

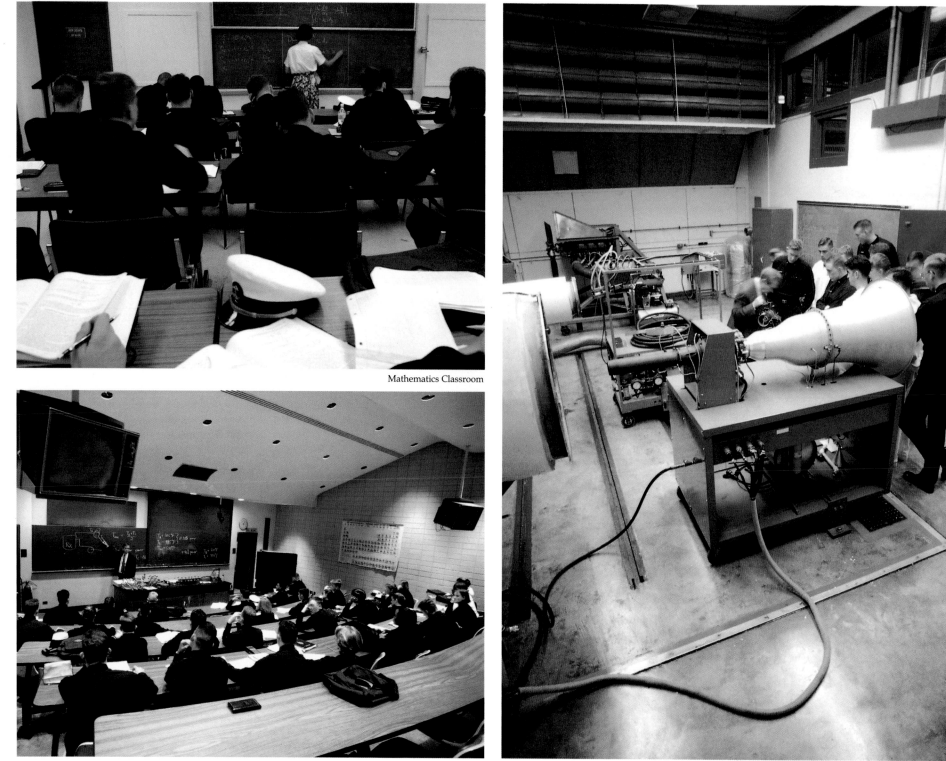

Mathematics Classroom

Chemistry Lecture

Jet Propulsion Lab

Modern warfare is as much a process of information gathering and processing as it is a clash of arms. The Naval Academy has a goal of preparing officers who can manage data in a technology-driven Navy and Marine Corps. Classrooms are equipped with systems like the Navy Tactical Wargaming Center, which creates a "virtual" combat experience. Of course, mechanical training, like in the gas turbine lab (right) is also computer-intensive.

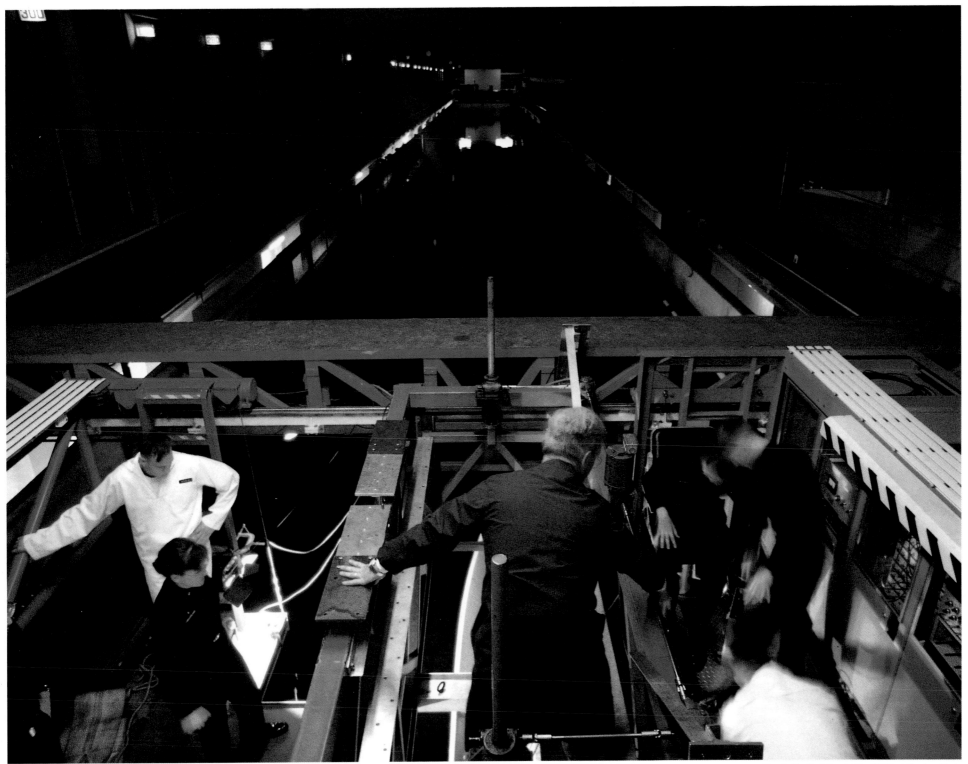

Hands-On Training At the 320 Foot Towing Tank

Ship design and ship handling is taught in either of the Naval Academy's two towing tanks: a 120-foot tank and a huge 320-foot tank. Naval architecture majors participate in a fully-integrated program of field training, hands-on laboratory work and the latest in computer-aided ship design. Additional tanks simulate a circulating water channel and a static stability environment. Midshipmen learn to weigh the many conflicting requirements in the process of designing a complex end product – a modern ship.

It isn't enough just to be competitive aboard one of the Academy's specialized Ocean racers. The sailing program exists to "provide midshipmen with opportunities to develop leadership as well as seamanship skills." Sailors compete in single-handed Laser sailboats (15 feet long) as well as part of the 14-man crew shown above. The Robert Crown Sailing Center on the Severn River consistently turns out top-ranked individual and team racers.

Training in all aspects of navigation, from celestial to that employing modern satellite positioning systems, is an important part of Academy life. Above, students learn to use the ancient sextant. Navigational instruction begins during Plebe Summer and continues as part of the Yard's integrated professional training.

Seamanship Begins With Sailing

Midshipmen Stationed With The Fleet

Summers Are Spent On Naval Ships

Sailing On Naval 44's

During Plebe Summer every midshipman is required to participate in seamanship training aboard several different sailing vessels used at the academy. After this, approximately one third of the midshipmen sign up for CSNTS advanced seamanship training where they will spend extended periods sailing the Bay and to other East coast ports. Each summer the midshipmen are rotated to various bases around the world for hands-on experience with the fleet. This includes flying in Navy aircraft at Pensacola, diving in nuclear submarines and enduring battlefield conditions in mock engagements led by Marine Corp instructors.

Free Rappelling From a Helicopter

Not every Academy graduate goes on to walk steel decks. Some choose careers in the Marine Corps, and are awarded a Second Lieutenant's commission at graduation. Those who make this choice attend a rigorous four week officer candidate course in Quantico, Virginia, with a follow-up assignment to a Fleet Marine Force unit. With this in mind, midshipmen are exposed to all aspects of military service. Some of this includes sail and power seamanship, rappelling from helicopters and firearms training.

Midshipmen March Before Kick-Off

Parachute Demonstration Before The Game

Cheerleaders Inspire The Brigade

Navy Carries The Ball

The annual Army-Navy game is perhaps the most hard-fought rivalry in collegiate football. Academy teams have played in every major bowl game in the country, and many players have gone on to hall-of-fame quality professional careers after completing their military commitment. There are twenty-nine other varsity teams, and participation on a varsity, club or intramural sport is a requirement of every midshipman.

Navy Football is One of 30 Varsity Sports Offered

"At the Naval Academy, the athletic program is not just an extracurricular activity, it is part of the mission and as such receives a priority much different than a civilian school...Athletics can provide leadership opportunities, and the experience of team play, cooperative effort, commitment and individual sacrifice for goals...Athletics are a big part of every midshipman's life at the Naval Academy." *Jack Lengyel, Director of Athletics* The parapets at Navy-Marine Corps Stadium are emblazoned with the names of naval engagements in which Academy alumni have given their lives: Sicily, Normandy, Iwo Jima, Quang Tin.

Herndon Before It Is Besieged

Spectators Cheer On the Plebes

Replacing the Cap

Herndon Monument - On the morning of the first day of Commissioning Week upperclassmen place a plebe "dixie cup" cap atop Herndon Monument and then grease the obelisk with 200 pounds of lard. That afternoon the Plebe class must together scale the monument and replace the cap with an officer's cover. This rite of passage signifies that their first year is thankfully over. Fourth classmen are no longer plebes, and will soon begin their second year at the Academy with a summer excursion aboard a Navy Yard Patrol Craft.

Herndon Monument - In a peculiar way, the effort required to ascend the slippery Herndon Monument is what Plebe Year is all about. Many of these midshipmen would have had neither the physical ability nor the team skills to accomplish this seemingly-jocular goal. Reaching the top is a victory for the entire Plebe class, and a symbol of the "tangible and intangible qualities that make an outstanding naval officer." It is said that the plebe who replaces the cap will be the first admiral from the class.

Midshipmen Line Up On Worden Field For Color Parade

Commissioning Week is marked by a furious series of activities for the midshipmen. The week begins with the traditional climb of the Herndon Monument marking the passage of the plebes to midshipmen. The week ends with the graduation ceremony of the senior class. They receive their Bachelor of Science degrees and at the same time are commissioned as officers in the Navy or Marine Corps.

Wedding At Naval Academy Chapel

Assembling For Color Parade

Wedding Family and Friends At Gazebo

Underclass Midshipmen At Graduation

Commissioning Week marks the end of four years of tremendous effort for the graduating class. Many of the new officers march right from the graduation ceremony to a wedding ceremony at the Naval Chapel, as they are not allowed to marry while a midshipman. At this time of year, the number of weddings at the chapel require them to be scheduled and performed with military precision.

Color Parade on Worden Field marks the yearly competition for the honor of being the Color Company. The entire student body of the Naval Academy makes up the Brigade of Midshipmen. The Brigade is divided into six Battalions each of which has five companies, for a total of thirty companies.

Color Parade is the culmination of the year long competition between the thirty companies. Points are accumulated for academic, professional and intramural achievements. This builds company spirit and teamwork. The highest scoring unit is named Color Company and, for the next year, will have the honor of representing the Naval Academy at official functions such as presidential inaugurations.

Commencement Address

Blue Angels Flyover

Presentation of Degrees

Graduation Held In Stadium

Graduation - Commissioning Week, the annual celebration of the success of yet another Academy graduating class, is the highlight of the year at The Yard, and an event which involves the entire Annapolis community. The Blue Angels flyover adds to the excitement and the majesty of the day. For all in the graduating class, this moment represents the highest achievement of their young lives. Degrees have been presented by revered Naval heroes, Secretaries of the Navy and even Presidents.

Graduation - This senior class has no more use for the midshipmen's hats they have worn for the last four years. Their graduation and commissioning, as either Ensigns in the Navy or Second Lieutenants in the Marine Corps entitles them to wear the officers' hats of those branches. The celebratory hat toss in Navy-Marine Corps Stadium is an Academy tradition.

Spa Creek At Sunset

A marina in Eastport rings with the sound of halyards snapping against aluminum masts as this armada of pleasure craft sit docked in the harbor. Across Spa Creek the dome of the State House is the ever-present sentinel for historic Annapolis.

CONTEMPORARY ANNAPOLIS

Throughout the nineteenth century and well into the twentieth, Annapolis sat quietly on the shores of the Chesapeake Bay without rattling a saber or rocking a boat (except the ceremonial swords behind the walls of the Academy and the rust-streaked workboats in the harbor). The Industrial Revolution passed her by.

Thankfully. Without the prosperity of other capitals, Annapolis and its rich legacy of brick and mortar was left to stand threadbare sentinel to the glorious past. During the legislative session the town came briefly back to life, only to sink again into a nine-month nap. Its mansions, its tiny working class rowhouses, its colonial warehouses, its churches and its academic halls never gave way to "progress," so that in 1952 when Historic Annapolis, Inc. turned its attention to preservation it found an abundance of possibilities.

That architectural serendipity sets the table that is modern Annapolis. It is but a ten-minute stroll from the City Market adjacent to the harbor to Church Circle, but the explorer is likely to pass a hundred or more historic houses on the way. George Washington called Annapolis "the genteelest city in North America," and this grace is reflected in the buildings which Historic Annapolis has saved. The Paca House, an imposing Georgian home built by one of Maryland's signers to the Declaration of Independence, was scheduled for demolition when it was saved in 1965. It now hosts emissaries from around the world who are visiting nearby Washington.

Surely the Georgian period was the pinnacle of the architect's art in Annapolis, which remains one of the nation's preeminent collections of 18th century buildings. Facing each other across Maryland Avenue are two venerable examples. The Hammond-Harwood House claims to be the most beautiful Georgian home in America, an assertion easily defensible. Merchant Matthias Hammond hired famous architect William Buckland to design his new home in 1774, ostensibly a gift for his fiancee. Before the mansion was finished, however, the young lady had bolted with a new suitor. Hammond died a bachelor a decade later.

The taller Chase-Lloyd House kept its harbor vista only because of Hammond's propriety. Samuel Chase, Maryland's most grandiloquent signer of the Declaration went broke trying to erect his ostentatious home. Edward Lloyd took advantage of Chase's misfortune, but when Hammond announced a three-story house right across dusty Maryland Avenue, Lloyd feared for the loss of his view. He offered to pay for wings on either side of the new villa if Hammond would settle for just two stories. A handshake, and the deal was struck.

But it is not just the finest mansions that have benefitted. Radiating uphill from the harbor, Pinkney, Cornhill and Fleet Streets are fronted by tiny clapboard homes, some no more than ten feet wide. All are pristinely restored. The idea that everything that has withstood centuries of neglect is important has been received jubilantly here.

So as we enter a new millennium, visitors flock to Annapolis, as they have for centuries, because it recognizes its place in history. Many buildings serve the same purposes they always have. Historic Inns of Annapolis has restored and opened several ancient hostelries and the Governor Calvert House, on State Circle welcomes guests as it has since the Revolution. The kitchen at Middleton's Tavern serves traditional fare to hungry visitors, while other early restaurants now feature menus with French, Italian and even Mexican selections. There's no place better than the stalls in the City Market, on the same site since 1788, for a plate of raw oysters, a bountiful sandwich, or Thomas Jefferson's favorite desert: ice cream.

In the summer, the Annapolis Garden Theatre stages Broadway shows in what was once a blacksmith shop on Victualling Street. For the more serious music lover there is the Annapolis Symphony, the Annapolis Opera, the Annapolis Ballet, the Annapolis Chorale and the world-renown Annapolis Brass Quintet. Popular plays come to life at stage of the Colonial Players on East Street and the Children's Theatre of Annapolis.

Post-Revolutionary Annapolitans suffered through a drought of the luxuries which were compulsory for their stylish lifestyles - indulgences which had been eagerly provided by London merchants. Things have returned to normal on Annapolis streets. Window-shoppers on both sides of Main Street are treated to wares from around the world - a potpourri of the most up-to-date fashions, glittering gifts, delicacies from truffles to chocolates to Bordeaux. Antique shops line Maryland Avenue south of State Circle, punctuated by galleries and craft shops. Surrounding the harbor are shops to serve the needs of sailors, or just those who like to wear bright yellow foul weather gear and decorate their homes with nautical prints.

Just across the Spa Creek bridge it is another country - the "Maritime Republic of Eastport." You won't have to have a passport in hand to make the crossing (though you can pick one up at several local merchants). Eastport has long been the local capital of the serious waterman, and while the bars of Annapolis are elbow-to-elbow in L.L. Bean, those just across the bridge are just as thickly peopled by oilcloth and gumboots. "We hold these truths to be self-evident," states the Eastport Declaration of Independence. "All men and women are created equal - as evidenced by the fact that, no matter their social or economic status, they all wear the same beat-up deck shoes."

The tongue-in-cheek nation's first "Prime Minister" was the local barber. "We are a friendly Republic, and will throw open our borders to any alien who wants to spend money here" he pledged at his inaugural. Laid-back is the word of the day in Eastport's cafes, taverns, restaurants and the many craft shops and galleries that dot the republic's streets. While Annapolis legislators discourse on various high-minded issues, Eastporters declare "we have full power to levy war, declare peace...and especially to throw really big Parties."

If day-to-day Annapolis isn't enough to satisfy, the calendar is filled with festivals. Early October welcomes the U.S. Sailboat Show, followed closely with the U.S. Powerboat Show. There are house tours and open houses throughout the year, some by candlelight. The opulent Paca House Gardens, and nearby Historic London Town and Gardens welcome enthusiasts to several horticultural fetes in spring and summer.

So if our first President magically returned to Annapolis after an absence of two hundred years he would approve of what he found. Well, maybe not the year-round bustle, and certainly not modern feminine attire, but George would happily savor the city's cuisine and enjoy its gregarious citizens. He would be comfortable at a room at the Maryland Inn (probably warmer in the winter and surely cooler in the summer). He would find much of the debate at the State House eerily familiar.

In short, he might wonder why he stayed away so long.

In 1970 a group of local businessmen decided to host the first U.S. Sailboat Show. Without a building large enough to hold all the shiny fiberglass sailboats they expected, the organizers decided to display the boats in the water. Every restaurant in Annapolis ran out of food the first night of the show. Today, as this view of (bottom to top) Back Creek, Spa Creek and the Severn River illustrates, every summer weekend is a Sailboat Show.

Spa Creek - When people hear "Spa Creek" most think of the bridge and the area around City Dock, but in Annapolis being "up the creek" can be a good thing. A bit inland along the quiet twists and turns of Spa Creek and Back Creek are homes, condos, marinas and boatyards. At their docks and slips one will find moored just about any type of boat imagined. It is tranquil views like this which is why people love Annapolis.

A forest of masts rises from the waters of Ego Alley off of Spa Creek near the foot of Main Street. As if to remind those in modern fiberglass boats that Annapolis has three hundred years of waterfront history, a reproduction of a lone gas street light will soon be casting shadows on the moored boats beneath it.

Ego Alley At City Dock

Prime real estate in Annapolis for boaters is the narrow passage at the City Dock area, euphemistically called "Ego Alley."
Sixty years ago the boats that occupied these slips were the rust-streaked. Today, the boats seem to get larger, more
luxurious and more numerous ever year. "Ego Alley" is an apt nickname for the area. It comes from the skippers of
large boats who wish to impress pedestrians by cruising in the narrow waterway seeking dockage where all can see,
and then the challenge of turning around without scuffing their hulls on the bulkhead – or another boat.

99

Sailors Visit Annapolis From Near and Far

During the sailing season many Annapolis visitors arrive by water, and with their folding carts walk into town to restock their galleys and their on-board wine cabinets. Annapolis is a leading East Coast destination for serious sailors, alongside Newport, Rhode Island and Ft. Lauderdale, Florida.

100

St. Anne's Towers Over Main Street

The narrow streets of the historic district can easily clog with traffic on a sunny weekend. Main street is lined with shops and restaurants to serve the city's guests, be they motorists or sailors. During some events such as the annual Boat Shows and Commissioning Week, it is a good idea to put your car in the first available garage or public lot and enjoy scenic Annapolis by walking to your destination.

State Circle Area - Looking over the flowers on State Circle are the shops and restaurants along Maryland Avenue. Hospitality is the name of the game here and whether one is seeking antiques, a good meal, lodging or a modern boutique it can be found on State Circle or one of its sidestreets which set out from the circle like spokes of a wheel. As the visitor wanders further from the circle, the shops become interspersed with historic houses. Continuing on you will probably find yourself at the gate of the Naval Academy or the waterfront, depending on which "spoke" you followed.

State Circle Area - During the busiest time in Annapolis - the three months early in the year when the Maryland legislature is in session - it is nearly impossible to get a dinner table anywhere in the vicinity of State Circle without a longstanding reservation. As the weather warms, however, and the legislators go back to Cambridge, Bel Air, Rockville or Oakland hungry patrons move to tables with the best view of all. Were any of these diners to look over their shoulder they would see the State House dome.

The Annapolis Marriott Waterfront is the only hotel in the heart of historic downtown Annapolis located directly on the water. Many of the guestrooms feature private balconies overlooking the Annapolis harbor and City Dock, with stunning views of the Chesapeake Bay. The hotel's restaurant is one of Annapolis' premier waterfront establishments, offering patrons alfresco dining on the waterfront deck or in the elegant nautical pub. The Chesapeake Ballroom is one of the most popular wedding venues on the East coast; it accommodates corporate meetings, Naval Academy affairs and many local events as well.

The dock of the **Annapolis Marriott Waterfront Hotel** is the berth for the 74 foot schooner Woodwind. This magnificently designed sailboat is available to the public for two-hour sailing cruises, as well as for private charters. After ending the cruise, many visitors enjoy a meal at the hotel restaurant. Whether from the restaurant deck or from their rooms, guests of the hotel enjoy various stunning views of Spa Creek, Ego Alley, Eastport and the Naval Academy.

Phillips Annapolis Harbor, located on the historic Annapolis City Dock, is the newest addition to the Phillips Family of Seafood Restaurants. Founded on tradition, Phillips has been serving authentic Maryland Style Seafood to guests in the Mid Atlantic since 1956. Phillips is a Maryland based, family owned and operated business with its roots firmly placed along the waters of the Chesapeake Bay.
At Phillips You Can Taste The Tradition ... Since 1956

View of City Dock Area During Boatshow

Annapolis shines during the U.S. Sailboat Show in October. Depending on the depth of one's pocketbook, there are boats from 8-foot sailing dinghies to one-hundred-foot-plus offshore cruisers. Snarling powerboats ("stink-potters" according to dedicated sailboat owners, who are not-so-affectionately called "rag-baggers" by their motoring counterparts) move in for the U.S. Powerboat Show a week later.

107

Chart House Restaurant is located on Spa Creek in the Eastport section of Annapolis. The restaurant occupies the former Annapolis Yacht Yard and John Trumpy & Sons boathouse. From the early 1900's to 1974, wooden submarine chasers, Vosper PT boats and Trumpy luxury yachts were built and maintained in the historic boathouse. Its open beam construction and 40 foot ceilings offer uncompromising views of the Annapolis Historic District, the Maryland State House and the U.S. Naval Academy. Chart House restored the dilapidated boathouse in 1979 and has since become a favorite among locals and visitors alike.

Spa Creek Bridge Connects Eastport, top, With Downtown Annapolis

Eastport - The area of Annapolis known as Eastport is a peninsula with Spa Creek on one side and Back Creek on the other. In the late 1800's what was farmland for centuries became home to watermen, tradesmen and boat builders. Western European immigrants and African Americans settled and worked there as Eastport turned into the center of Annapolis' growing maritime industry. The Spa Creek Bridge was built to connect it with "mainland" Annapolis. Today the maritime industry remains prevalent, but Eastport is a dynamic community with a diverse mix of people, trade and professional business, art, recreation and entertainment - and they seem to blend just fine.

109

Cocktail Bar and Lounge Area

The Capital Room

The Chesapeake Room

Ruth's Chris Steak House - Nestled in the quaint, quiet neighborhood of Eastport, on Severn Avenue - just across the bridge from the historic City Dock - Ruth's Chris Steak House is the premier dining destination in Annapolis. Ruth's Chris Steak House features aged, corn-fed, never frozen, USDA Prime steaks (served sizzling), live Maine lobster, fresh seafood and an extensive wine list. All in a sophisticated atmosphere highlighted by dark wood paneling, stained glass windows, nautical-themed etched glass wall inserts and paintings. The result, an invitingly elegant ambience that's suitable for special occasion and casual diners alike.

View Across Spa Creek From City Dock

"The Maritime Republic of Eastport" and "Eastportoricans" is how the people there refer to their home and themselves (this explains all the "MRE" bumper stickers and signs in the land across the creek). Eastport is unique to Annapolis in its culture and lifestyle. The atmosphere is relaxed and many find Eastport a welcome escape from the hustle and bustle of downtown Annapolis. The locals may sum it up best: Some said the essentials of life in Eastport are, "a good hat, good dog, good boat" and one bartender said, "There's no life beyond the bridge," tongue-in-cheek, referring to the Spa Creek Bridge that leads to Annapolis.

Main Dining Room With View Of Naval Academy And Spa Creek

O'Learys Seafood Restaurant - an icon of the Eastport maritime community - has been serving the freshest seafood and shell fish available for more than seventeen years. Visitors from around the globe seek out delicacies created from seafood rarely seen at other venues, matched only by the superb pairings of an expertly crafted wine list. Set in the historic waterfront Sadler residence, the contemporary mustard hues of the interior dance with the spectrum of golden colors at sunset in the main dining room.

"Two score and seven years ago, we the people of **Eastport** were annexed against our will into the City of Annapolis...we now do declare our independence and thereby do celebrate the unique maritime character of our own culture, our own history, our own horticulture, architecture and naval architecture, our people and our retrievers and felines, our own neighborhood, our own Eastport!" An excerpt from *The Eastport "Declaration of Independence", 1998*

Historic building markers are located throughout the National Historic Landmark District of Annapolis. Not only do the markers assist visitors in identifying houses with historic value, they encourage preservation of important structures. The centerpiece of the marker is the Liberty Tree, a tulip poplar that was over four hundred years old when it had to be removed from the campus of St. John's College in 1999. The various colors of the plaques identify different styles and ages of the homes. A list explaining each of them is available from the Historic Annapolis Foundation at the Shiplap House or the Paca House.

A May Day Basket Hangs on the Door of a Historic Home

May Day flower baskets adorning the doors of Annapolis homes has been a tradition since 1956 when Mrs. Phillip Briscoe, the first president of the Garden Club of Old Annapolis-Towne, re-introduced it. The festival of May Day was first celebrated by the Romans who carried it with them into England. Over the years the British continued the celebration whereby it was introduced to Annapolis during colonial times. Each May Day the Garden Club members walk the streets of historic Annapolis and judge each basket. The winners receive ribbons and their creators are invited to the Garden Club's May Day Tea.

Restored Homes Are Proudly Maintained

Pinkney Street is one of the charming, narrow streets that winds its way up the hill from the harbor. Its narrow, weatherboarded houses were once the homes of Annapolis workers - stevedores, sailmakers, blacksmiths and ship carpenters.

The variety of housing in the historic district of Annapolis is extensive. It is not unusual to find a large brick colonial right next to a row of small brightly painted clapboard homes. Whatever the size or style, one can be assured the homes are meticulously maintained. This diversity reflects the more than 300 years of development and change which Annapolis has gracefully weathered.

Moe Hanson, Resident Artist

Ceramics Class

Painting Class

Painting Class

Maryland Hall for the Creative Arts is the rebirth of the former Annapolis High School. This adaptive re-use of a 1932 building evolved from a 1979 partnership formed by community arts advocates and the Anne Arundel County Board of Education to provide creative experiences through quality arts education and culturally diverse programs. The Auditorium, one of the area's largest public performing arts venues, serves more than 55,000 patrons yearly. Maryland hall offers studio space for thirteen professional artists-in-residence and numerous exhibits in its three galleries. Instructors conduct classes for all ages, in visual and performing arts, with more than 5,000 registrations annually.

"Tosca" by Giacomo Puccini

The Annapolis Opera, in its 27th year, emphasizes that Opera is now for everyone especially with the addition of electronic English translation (surtitles). Established in Maryland since 1752, Annapolis was the second opera house in the country. The present company produces two fully staged operas in their original language each season. Also presented are a holiday program, an opera for children, a Piccolo opera, a dinner opera and an annual vocal competition which allows 8 finalists the opportunity to sing with the Annapolis Opera in a future production. The Opera's "Students for Learning" program and Opera Appreciation courses enlighten both students and adults.

Jennifer Dancesia and Dmitry Malikov in "The Nutcracker"

Ballet Theatre of Annapolis was founded in 1980 by Artistic Director Edward Stewart and has grown to become Maryland's premier ballet company. It now stages four full-length productions a year at their resident theatre, Maryland Hall for the Creative Arts, and mini-performances at several other locations. The company currently features 22 dancers, including former principals from the Bolshoi Ballet and the National Ballet of China. The Ballet Theatre School provides The Russian Method of dance training to its students, several of which have been accepted by such prestigious schools as Alvin Ailey, Boston Ballet, Joffrey Ballet and Kirov Academy.

The Annapolis Symphony Orchestra in Concert

The Annapolis Symphony Orchestra, directed by Dr. Leslie B. Dunner (above right), is a fully professional organization performing at Maryland Hall for the Creative Arts. The orchestra offers a regular subscription series featuring renowned soloists and the finest symphonic repertoire, presented in Friday – Saturday evening concerts with free pre-concert lectures. In addition to Family, Holiday Pops, Summer Parks concerts and Chamber Concerts, the ASO offers an extensive array of educational programs that have attracted national attention and acclaim.

The Maryland Renaissance Festival, for nearly twenty-five years, has transformed a field in Crownsville, near Annapolis, to a 16th century village. King Henry VIII rises from the grave to eat, drink and be merry, while Will Shakespeare and his troupe perform in the theatre. It is often hard to tell the festival goers from the hosts as many come dressed in Renaissance period garb. But don't feel left out, you can rent costumes at the fair and join in the revelry.

Renaissance Festival - "By the Order of His Most Royal Majesty..."everyone is commanded to have a noble good time at the Maryland Renaissance Festival, held August through October each year. Ladies of the Court are on hand (gossiping, no doubt, about the King's new mistress, Anne Boleyn), there is jousting to watch (Maryland's state sport), crafts and artisans of all types and the kitchens prepare dishes worthy of a king for all to savor.

Helen Avalynne Tawes Garden is nestled amongst the state government buildings along Rowe Boulevard, just past the Navy-Marine Corp Stadium. The five acre garden recreates the various geographic areas of the state. As Maryland is called "America in Miniature," this garden is nicknamed "Maryland in Miniature." A visit is ideal, whether it is to examine the diverse flora or to enjoy the ponds while walking the footpaths. The park is named for Mrs. J. Millard Tawes, first lady of Maryland from 1959 to 1967.

Quiet Waters Park is just south of Historic Annapolis situated on the South River and Harness Creek. The park is 336 acres of both woodlands and open space with over six miles of hiking and cycling trails. There are six pavilions for picnicking and the Blue Heron Center is available for meetings, parties and weddings. Activities at the park are available year round from summer concerts and boating to ice skating in winter.

Two sloops reach for the next marker on a stiff starboard breeze. The Wednesday night regatta during sailing season means spirited competition among Annapolis sailors.

MARITIME TRADITIONS

On September 21, 1997, ten graceful, tall sailboats set out from South Hampton, England, embarking on a demanding, dangerous, exhilarating global journey called the Whitbread Round the World Race. Emblazoned on the hull of one was the grinning sea monster logo of Chessie Racing, the sponsor of Chessie, a seven million dollar, high tech sloop that put Annapolis on the international sailing map. The launch of Chessie and her successful finish eight months later capped a three-century tradition of seafaring from the little town where the South and Severn Rivers enter the Chesapeake Bay.

"From my viewpoint 100 feet above the water it feels like we are flying - literally...Chasing fronts and sailing on the edge makes this a race without equal," wrote one Chessie crewmember as the sloop approached Capetown, South Africa at the end of leg one. Generations of Annapolis-based sailors probably felt the same exhilaration, but from atop the main on a coasting schooner filled with lumber, a skipjack dredging oysters or a bugeye hauling watermelons to Baltimore. Water is the history of Annapolis, the reason anyone came here in the first place, and the reason we continue visiting.

The tiny harbor has always been the focal point of the town. Every street radiates from the harbor outward - to State and Church Circles, to the Naval Academy, to the fine brick homes of Revolutionary patriots, to the rest of America. Colonial Governor Francis Nicholson recognized this fact when he moved the capital here in 1695. Anne Arundel Town was already a burgeoning port for the export of tobacco and one of the most important Chesapeake ports of call. The merchants who fueled the local economy watched their tobacco-laden ships depart and saw the same return filled with English goods from the top floors of their townhouses. Smaller boats skipped across the Bay, serving the villages of the Eastern Shore. Later, steamboats called in Annapolis to take passengers and goods to hundreds of points up and down the Bay.

Today, most waterborne visitors have come here for fun, not to sell a load of muddy Chesapeake oysters or feisty blue crabs. The halyards that sing across the harbor as they chatter against aluminum masts raise sails on pleasure boats, not wooden workboats. Their compartments are filled with champagne rather than tobacco. The bass line is provided by growling power yachts as they make their way to the Chesapeake. Annapolis, alongside Newport, Rhode Island and Fort Lauderdale, Florida, is a major East Coast yachting capital.

In recent memory the slips now occupied by boats with names like "Miss Behavin'" or "Liquid Asset" were filled with rust-streaked local boats called the "Purnell T. White" and the "Edna and Maud." Wagons converged on the harbor daily to unload the bounty of the Bay, much of which ended up on tables at Middleton's, just a few steps away, but some which traveled as far as the Fulton Fish Market on New York's Battery. But as ports with accommodations for larger craft, or more expeditious locations eclipsed the Annapolis waterfront, and as demand for dockage by well-heeled yachtsmen drove up costs, these slips were abandoned by working watermen and adopted by the Docksider set.

Annapolis quickly adjusted, welcoming anyone who arrives by water whether it is to refuel his skipjack's pushboat or to refuel the wine cabinet in the galley of his Trumpy 60-footer. A complete array of marine services is available for weekend navigators. There are boat brokers who can fill one's appetite for anything from a 16-foot catamaran to a five-room houseboat. Charters are available for "bare-boaters" (where you are your own captain) or luxury cruises where the professional captain also probably prepares a mean crab imperial and mixes a perfect bloody.

Hanging on racks at local Annapolis shops one can find the latest boating regalia, and in Eastport one can find the best waterproof workboots and yellow slickers. "We specialize in sailing platters," boasts an Annapolis caterer, while a local nautical gift shop advertises itself as the "Tiffany's of Annapolis." Shops edging the harbor are filled with all manner of boating necessities, from complete global satellite systems to floating bottle openers.

It was, of course, no accident that the Naval Academy relocated here from Philadelphia in 1845. Proximity to the Chesapeake Bay provided the perfect body of water to introduce young sailors to life on the water and the relatively well-protected harbor provided Academy vessels with sanctuary from the periodic nor'easters which rake the East Coast. Ships of the modern Navy long ago grew beyond the ability of Annapolis to sustain them, but dozens of training boats from the Yard still cruise the waters just off the mouth of the Severn.

If one wishes to learn sailing without the nine-year commitment of the Naval Academy, there are several schools which can give the landlubber a good grounding in boat handling, rules of the water, and maritime safety in just one weekend. Basic sailing classes often use the locally-designed "Rainbow", a small stable sloop that is perfect for the fledgling skipper. Cruising classes take place aboard a selection of larger boats, stopping at Oxford, St. Michaels and other Chesapeake points while learning the art of cruising on the sometimes-unpredictable Bay.

Waterfront activities fill the calendar in Annapolis and Eastport. Boating season unofficially begins with the Maryland Marine Trade Expo in April. The Bay Bridge Boat and Yacht Sale follows shortly thereafter. St. John's College sponsors the Waterfront Arts Festival in June, a three-day event celebrating area visual and performing artists. In early October the harbor hosts the U.S. Sailboat Show, and within a week the U.S. Powerboat Show comes to town. Chesapeake Appreciation Days, centered on nearby Sandy Point State Park, bring together the remaining boats of the Chesapeake Bay skipjack fleet together for a hotly contested, but convivial race. Informal events include the Wednesday night race series, which throughout the sailing season can draw a hundred or more competitors. The races can be watched from the harbor.

There is no excuse not to feel like a sailor in Annapolis, even if the pinnacle of one's maritime ambitions is a day in Uncle Red's rowboat, or if the total of boating experience is four years in the Coast Guard at the helm of a dishwasher. The "Harbor Lady" leaves often daily for a forty-minute tour of points beyond - beyond the cluster of communication towers at the mouth of the harbor, that is. Other cruises cross the Bay for just a day, mimicking the steamboats that once took holiday revelers to the beach resorts of Tolchester and Betterton on the Eastern Shore.

Plenty of Annapolitans and guests prefer to feel the solid wooden floors of a local drinkery beneath their feet rather than rolling wooden decks. Even here there is an abundance of sailing experience to be enjoyed. One can get a tan almost as easily at an outdoor table as on the foredeck, after all. And the water will be nearly as close.

With every square foot of sail possible catching a downwind breeze, these boats round a marker on a Wednesday sail. Bright spinnakers will be quickly dropped as they point upwind for the next leg. This may not be the America's Cup, but it is very serious racing.

Sailing the waters around Annapolis, one is likely to see one or more boats from the Naval academy fleet amongst the everyday boaters. Pictured above is one of the larger racing vessels. Along with 24 of these larger boats including Navy 44's, the fleet has over 100 Lasers, 22 FJ's, 22 420's, 14 J/24's and 28 Knock Abouts.

The skipper watches his spinnaker catch the breeze on what appears to be a calm race night. No doubt there are crews this particular Wednesday looking aloft and begging for "some weather." Sailors always prefer to have wind, but times like this allow the normally intense race teams to enjoy the tranquility that can be found on the water.

To the casual observer, it is hard to make heads or tails of a sailboat race. Every boat is seemingly headed in a different direction (indeed sometimes they are), but all are intent on the same goal – to navigate the course and reach the finish line in as short a time as possible. Sailing skill is always a factor, but often a correct guess on a wind shift or a bit of plain luck may determine the winner.

As the gun goes off on the Committee Boat, racers jockey for position to cross the starting line (top right). Little is more chaotic than the start of a sailboat race. In a brisk breeze, boats heel sharply while crew members cling to the windward rail to keep the vessel upright.

As the sun sets behind the Naval Academy several sailboats head inland. By lingering for the view they will end up docking and stowing sails in the dark. These sailors will tell you, however, it's more than worth it having had the best seat in the house for a spectacular Annapolis sunset.

The view from the top of the mast is truly exciting. The sails seem to grow larger while the deck below recedes to a mere spot on the water. Some find the height and lack of a solid platform intimidating, so it helps if the repairs that are needed go easily. There are others who enjoy the experience and go up just for the view.

There are times when it becomes necessary to don a safety harness, attach oneself to a heavy steel cable and go up the mast. Usually this is when some type of repair needs to be made while under way: a sail may be hung up, the upper rigging may need adjustment or a halyard may need to be retrieved. There are occasions in light air when someone will be hoisted up the mast to look for the elusive wind.

From the shore it is difficult to even tell where the finish line is. At the start of the race, the line is but two points on the water until the Committee Boat has raced to one of its ends. If you thought the start was pandemonium, watch as boats, under a full press of nylon, sprint for the finish. This one will be reenacted hundreds of times tonight over the rails of boats rafted together or in Annapolis and Eastport bars.

Gary Jobson Sails His 28' Herreshoff Design on Spa Creek

Gary Jobson, one of America's premier sailors, has resided in Annapolis since 1977 when he came to coach the U.S. Naval Academy Sailing Team. His sailing achievements, on and off the water, are too numerous to list. Presently he is ESPN's sailing commentator and spends much of his time promoting sailing worldwide through Jobson Sailing, Inc. Gary was awarded the Herreshoff Trophy by U.S. Sailing for significant contribution to the sport of sailing. Interestingly, his own boat is built from a 1932 Herreshoff design. When Gary's schedule allows, one is just as likely to see him cruising on Spa Creek as any other local sailor.

With all the boating and waterfront activity on and around Spa Creek, it is sometimes easy to miss its serene beauty, especially at sunset. Nightfall is upon the town and most of the boats were docked hours ago. Their captains and crew are off enjoying food and drink in a favorite restaurant or pub. This quiet time by the water, as the city lights begin to glisten across the harbor, is one of the reasons people are drawn to Annapolis and why some decide to stay.

Fireworks light the night sky over the Annapolis harbor during an Independence Day celebration. The Fourth of July has a special meaning in Annapolis, a town that played such a seminal role in the establishment of the nation over two hundred years ago.

"Chessie" Leaves Annapolis in the 1997-98 Whitbread Race

Bruce Farr, right, and Russell Bowler, left, Design Volvo 60 Hull Using FastShip™by Proteus Engineering

Design Meeting With Bruce Farr, Russell Bowler (standing); Jim Schmicker, and Stephen Morris (seated)

Farr Yacht Design, Ltd., the world's leading designer of high-performance racing yachts, has been based in Eastport since 1981. New Zealand born owners Bruce Farr and Russell Bowler and a team of 11 employees makeup Farr Yacht Design, a company with the most extensive resumes of winning race results ever compiled by the yachts of a single design group. Their long-running record of achievement includes 34 World Championships and a multitude of victories at internationally prestigious grand prix yachting events such as the Whitbread Round the World Race, Admiral's Cup and many others.

Among **Farr Yacht Design's** many achievements is the creation of the popular Farr 40 One Design Class, built by Carroll Marine. Steve Kaminer's Farr 40 OD, *Predator* (pictured above), is a regular participant in Annapolis Yacht Club's Wednesday Night Racing Series. The Farr 40 One Design class is managed and marketed by Farr Yacht Design's sister company, Farr International, Inc., which is also based in Eastport. Farr International was founded in 1982 by Bruce Farr, Russell Bowler and company President, Geoffrey Stagg. In addition to managing several Farr one-design classes, Farr International specializes in yacht brokerage and project management for Farr designs.

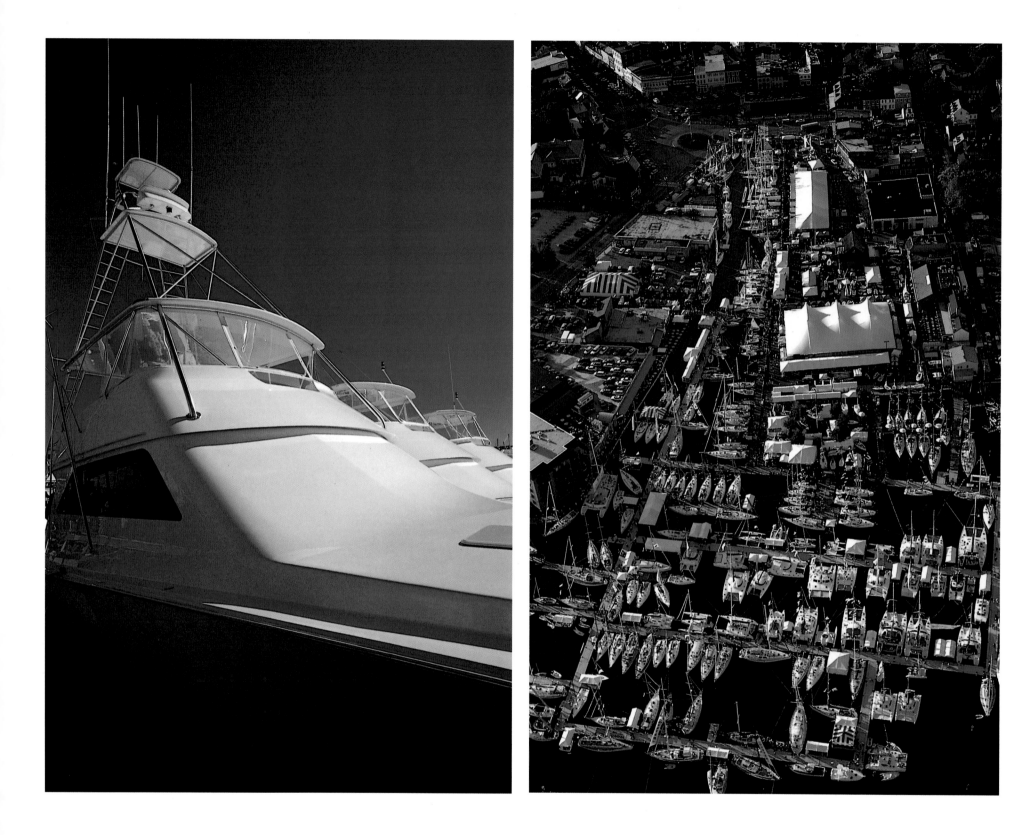

Early October brings the **U.S. Sailboat Show** to Annapolis (right). The notion that a floating show would be a success, rather than a coliseum full of boats on platforms, was revolutionary when the first show took place in 1970. The following weekend the **U.S. Powerboat Show**, which had its debut in 1972, takes the same berths in the Annapolis and Eastport harbors.

When the powerboats move into the harbor, one finds outriggers and flying bridges rising into the air rather than aluminum masts. Whether looking for a 10 foot run-about, a 50 foot sportfisher or a 100 plus foot ocean-going yacht, there is something for everyone on display. Accessories, standard and custom, are also available, with the amenities for one's boat limited only by the depth of their pockets.

Refinish and Painting of an Older Boat

Beginning Construction of a Express Cruiser

Belkov Yacht Company is the last remaining builder in Eastport providing yacht construction from design to launch. Opened in 1980, the company entered the yacht-finished workboat market refitting boats to improve comfort and recreational performance. Three years later Belkov launched its first original boat, based on a bay workboat called the Hooper Island Draketail. From that, the Belkov Picnic Express was developed - a much refined version of that first draketail launch. A reputation for quality keeps the business split between refitting/repair and new boat construction.

Not long ago, the Annapolis harbor - even "Ego Alley" - was crowded with the white, deadrise workboats that still put out to the Chesapeake in search of crabs, oysters and finfish. With the steering stick in hand, this captain motors in his traditional Chesapeake boat. The wide "washboards" along the rail enable him to stand while maneuvering a pair of eighteen-foot oyster tongs over the side.

Eastport protects its maritime heritage with special zoning regulations requiring waterfront zones to have at least 75% maritime use. This means everything from yacht building and repair to sailmaking, rigging, boat cabinetry and woodworking, yacht brokerages and marine publishing. The tools and methods may be different, but much of the same work was being done in the late 1800's when the first boatyards moved into Eastport. From 1920 to 1974 is considered its "Golden Era" when Eastport was known for some of the finest motor and sail powered vessels ever made.

The Raven Maritime Studio

Howard's Skilled Hands Work His Favorite Chisel

Raven Maritime Studio and its proprietor, Howard Rogers, are both fixtures in Eastport. Born in England, Howard trained as a shipwright joiner and became a London Guild Gold Medalist. Upon moving to the United States he turned his skills to more artistic pursuits. Today Howard is best known for his signs and boat nameboards, all carved and finished by hand, though his real passion is maritime paintings in watercolor and pen-and-ink. The studio at Severn and Second St. is worth a visit, as Howard is of a vanishing breed of craftsmen.

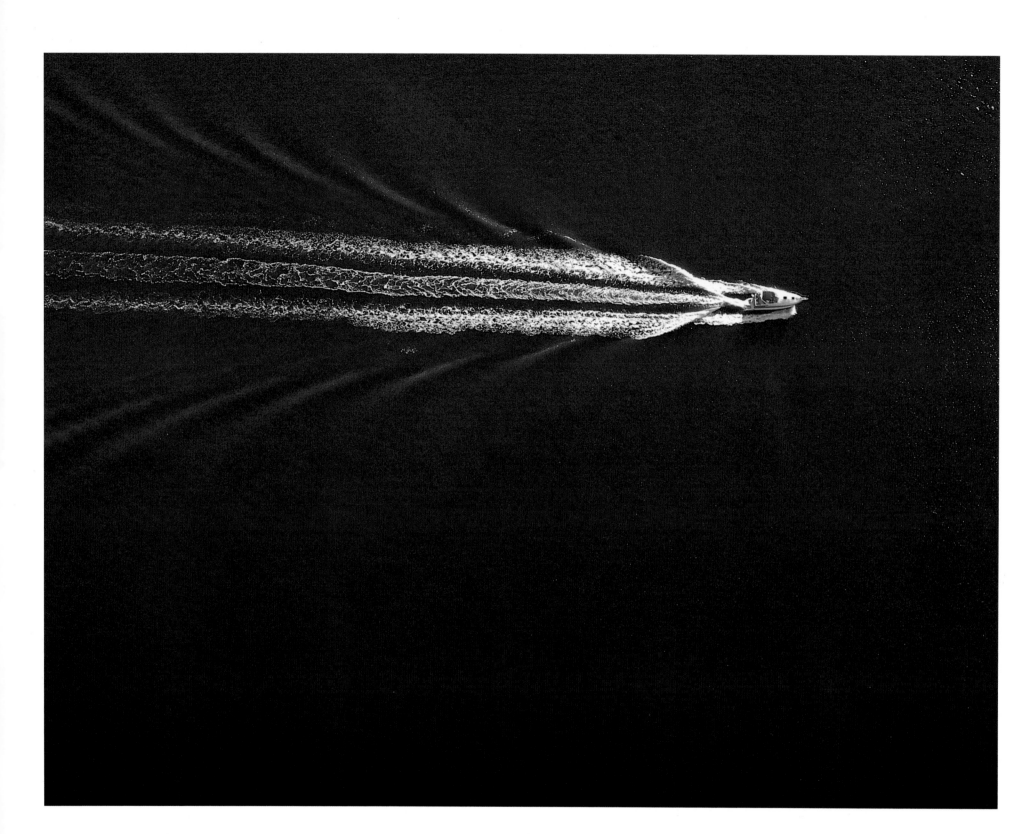

Leaving its wake emblazoned across the waters of the Severn River, a powerboat heads out for a day on the Chesapeake Bay. Annapolis may be known for its sailing, but there is a considerable powerboat set as well. Whether piloting a small skiff, a fully rigged offshore fisher or a million dollar luxury yacht, boaters value Annapolis for its safe harbors and easy access to the rest of the Bay.

Thomas Point Shoal Light Station has guarded the entrance to the South River since 1875. Screwpile lights like this once dotted the Chesapeake. Now it is the last active screwpile house on the Bay, warning sailors away from the shoal waters approaching Annapolis. The Thomas Point Light was automated in 1986, though keeper's quarters are maintained in the hexagonal structure. It is listed as a landmark on the National Register of Historic Places.

A container ship stacked high with cargo cruises past the Bay Bridge and the Severn River on its way to the Atlantic Ocean and overseas ports. Two hundred years ago it would have been a small wood boat, powered by sail, leaving from Annapolis not Baltimore. It was not until the ships got much larger that Baltimore's deep water drew them away. With a large part of its economy removed Annapolis did not wither, but adapted as it has many times in its history. Today, its port is filled with recreational craft from ski boats and daysailors to multi-million dollar yachts. The economic progression of Annapolis is indicative of the entire state of Maryland evolving as necessary to remain at the forefront of economic growth and success.

CORPORATE OVERVIEW

When Anne Arundel Town was christened Annapolis in the late 1600s, becoming the capital of the colony of the various Lords Baltimore, the economy of the town and the colony as a whole were closely linked to the water and the soil. Annapolis was chosen as the capital largely because of the proximity of the Chesapeake Bay and the rich tobacco fields of southern Maryland. Baltimore, just thirty miles to the north, was still just a handful of primitive buildings clustered around a yet-to-be-developed harbor. There was no national capital. Annapolis stood as great a chance of becoming an economic powerhouse as virtually any city in the New World.

Yet as one wanders the narrow streets of Annapolis and Eastport today it is obvious that this did not happen. Not long after the American Revolution the economic future of Annapolis was already determined, and it would not be to host major industrial, mercantile or agricultural interests. That burden would fall to other East Coast cities, to the long-term advantage of Annapolis. Her pristine streets, treasured collection of colonial buildings and peaceful way of life were preserved largely because the Industrial Revolution passed her by.

This is not to say that the state capital is any less economically important as we enter the 21st-century than she was in the days when her quays were piled high with hogsheads of tobacco and schooners anchored offshore, waiting for a berth. Three months out of every year, when lawmakers from across Maryland call Annapolis home, economic policy is hammered out which controls the destiny of everyone in the state, and affects those well beyond the Potomac River in the south and the Mason-Dixon line to the north. The legislature faces issues of development, growth, environmental impact, education and social policy – issues debated in statehouses everywhere. Many ideas hatched in Annapolis, most notably Maryland's dedication to "Smart Growth" (which marries business and residential growth to preservation of natural resources and the sustaining social fabric) as well as her nationally-recognized efforts to reverse the ecological destruction of the Chesapeake Bay have been copied in other state capitals.

Maryland sits near the southern end of the Washington-Boston corridor, the nation's most concentrated, busiest and most productive mercantile route – a passage which many would argue continues as far south as Atlanta. The Chesapeake Bay splits the state in half, providing a watery roadway that has made Baltimore a leading port of entry since the late eighteenth century. The huge freighters of modern times bypass the little harbor at the mouth of the Severn as they make their way to Baltimore's Patapsco River piers. Computerized cranes there lift thousands of cargo containers from the cavernous hulls of ships from all over the world, delivering automobiles from Japan and petroleum products that originated in the Middle East. But the policy that made the development of a world-class port in Baltimore possible was initiated in Annapolis, and when the state's financial and business leaders seek greater opportunity they often start in Annapolis too.

The state's economy today in a sense does not bear much resemblance to her early roots. Tobacco trade must have occupied a larger space on the annual legislative agenda in 1800 than it does in 2000. Technology, bio-medicine, tourism and services, education and transportation form the basis for Maryland's fiscal strength now. Professional and technical workers make up a fifth of the state workforce, the highest percentage of any state in the nation.

Maryland is the birthplace of modern railroads and the state is still criss-crossed by rails for the transport of goods and people. Trains passed Annapolis by in their hurry to link the industrial base of the Northeast to the agricultural interests of the South, insuring that it would remain a sleepy, well-preserved Bayfront town rather than another Baltimore or Philadelphia. The interstate highway system has done pretty much the same, and although Annapolis is tied to nearby Baltimore and Washington by modern expressways their existence did not encourage industry to seek out Anne Arundel County, or its seat at Annapolis, as potential sites for factories and warehouses.

So Annapolis is able to benefit from the general prosperity that Marylanders enjoy largely without suffering the depredation that comes with wholesale development. The state enjoys unheralded good fortune, with a household income that is 10% above the national average and unemployment that is always on the low end of the scale. Employment patterns have changed, and Maryland has adapted. Manufacturing jobs are in decline, especially in heavy industry, but aerospace and technology have more than made up the slack. The mining industry in Western Maryland employs but a fraction of the number it did at the close of the last century, and the canning industry has also declined. This has been balanced in part by a boom in the service sector, and tourism has provided jobs all across the state that didn't exist just twenty years ago.

Maryland's adaptability to the changing scene has come about with the cooperation of the private sector and the state government in Annapolis. Maryland's economic development programs have helped new businesses get off the ground, and that state has been a leader in the development of enterprise zones that offer various incentives and tax benefits to companies that choose to locate here. The business climate is constantly improving, and much of the credit belongs to those who guide its destiny from their desks in Annapolis.

The water is, of course, still a major attraction. Businesses consider recreational amenities and opportunity for personal growth when comparing one likely site to another, and Maryland is blessed with proximity to the Chesapeake Bay and the Atlantic beach at Ocean City, less than two hours from State Circle. One of the city's leading "businesses" (at least one of its largest employers) - the United States Naval Academy - didn't choose Annapolis because it was close to Washington or Baltimore.

On a smaller scale traditional businesses have prospered in Annapolis, and the city has adapted to the economic winds that have blown her through three centuries of history. There is still a powerful dependence on water, though it is to bring the thousands of pleasure craft that stop here seasonally rather than commercial ships that go to larger seaports elsewhere. The purchasing power of boat owners is not to be looked down upon, however, and their needs fuel a string of Annapolis businesses from restaurants to boatbuilders. Boat repair facilities dot the "Maritime Republic of Eastport," across the harbor from Annapolis proper and custom yachts are still built here from the ground up. Bars throughout the town are lined with sailors from spring through fall. Artists and craftspeople show their products in galleries in the historic area, and guitars manufactured locally are sought by fine musicians who play everything from the Delta Blues to Segovia.

Annapolis exerts an influence over the economic machine of Maryland that far exceeds her direct impact on the state's bottom line. It has been an arrangement that is uniquely mutually-beneficial. The town provides an ideal forum in which policy makers can develop strategy for economic growth beyond the tumult of big-city life. In a way, it reminds us from whence we came and gives us a solid ground from which we can better plan the future.

TCS Headquarters in Annapolis

TeleCommunication Systems, Inc. develops network application software and services that enable the delivery of Internet content, short messages and enhanced data communication services to a wide variety of wireless devices. TCS also provides communications engineering services, including the design and installation of complex information processing and telecommunication systems. Founded in 1987 by Naval Academy alumnus Maurice Tosé, TCS is an Annapolis, Maryland based company with more than 300 employees and a customer list which includes AT&T, Lucent Technologies and other leading wireless carriers, the State of Maryland and federal agencies. TCS is a nationally recognized minority business enterprise.

Capital-Gazette Newspapers has been publishing in Annapolis since 1727 and today publishes five newspapers in its modern plant, just off West Street, near Parole. The company's mission statement invokes the words of Joseph Pulitzer: "Every issue of every newspaper presents a battle for excellence." Owner and publisher Philip Merrill reaffirms that pledge: "From our more than 2,000 newspaper carriers to our more than 400 dedicated employees, the struggle for excellence continues each day." The company publishes The Capital (50,000 circulation daily), the Maryland Gazette (34,000 twice weekly) and these weeklies: The Bowie Blade-News (25,000), the Crofton News-Crier (10,000) and the West County News (15,000). The company's Web site, HometownAnnapolis.com, one of the first newspaper sites online, averages 250,000 hits per week.

ABS Headquarters In White Marsh, MD

On Site Technical Training

ABS Showroom Exhibits Full Product Line

Complete Product Inventory At Local Warehouse

ACTION BUSINESS SYSTEMS (ABS) - Since 1979 Action Business Systems has provided tens of thousands of businesses and institutions throughout Maryland with state-of-the-art, award winning copiers, printers, facsimiles, and digital equipment from its headquarters and showroom in White Marsh and locations in Annapolis, Arlington, Lanham, Waldorf and at the Ravens' PSINet stadium in Downtown Baltimore. Guided by founder Wm. B. Wallace, Jr.'s pioneering "We Care" philosophy, which guarantees total customer satisfaction, ABS is the only company to have been selected five times to the "Top 50" office equipment dealers in the United States.

The ABS Senior Management Team

Annapolis Office Conveniently Located At 151 West Street

ABS Maintains A Complete Parts Inventory

Latest Digital Equipment On Display In Annapolis Showroom

ACTION BUSINESS SYSTEMS' enviable 99% customer satisfaction rating and its commitment to the community through a variety of educational and hiring programs have earned ABS the distinction of receiving the Better Business Bureau's Torch Award for Business Ethics. In an industry measured by customer service response time, ABS has distinguished itself by maintaining a complete, in-house inventory of equipment, parts, and accessories which enable them to provide a 2-4 hour service response time. Designated as a Dealer Assisted Technical Education Center, ABS offers manufacturer authorized technical training at its headquarters. ABS also offers employees regular "We Care" customer satisfaction training in order to provide the highest level of customer service available.

Patient Gets Physical Therapy at the Center For Joint Replacement.

Mother Bonds With Infant in a Level III+ Neonatal Intensive Care Unit

AAMC Has An Active Community Outreach Program

Neurosurgeons at AAMC Use Vector Vision for Computer-Aided Surgery

Anne Arundel Medical Center has been rated among the nation's 100 top hospitals for orthopedics and has the fourth highest birth rate in Maryland, as well as a multi-dimensional oncology program. Expansion at the Medical Park includes a Vascular Institute, the Maryland Neurological Institute, a Diabetes Center and expanded services for cancer patients. AAMC has a medical staff of more than 600 and is the fourth largest private employer in Anne Arundel County.

Modern Helipad Adjacent To AAMC Medical Park Campus

In the fall of 2001, **Anne Arundel Medical Center** (AAMC) opened a new Acute Care Pavilion on its 28-acre campus near the Annapolis Mall. The move consolidated all AAMC healthcare at a single site, including a dedicated women's and children's center (Clatanoff Pavilion), outpatient surgery (Edwards Pavilion) and radiation oncology (Donner Pavilion) centers; and a diagnostic radiology facility, Breast Center and a comprehensive range of ambulatory health services (Sajak Pavilion).

Airport Communications Systems and Air Traffic Management Around the World

Military Engineering Services and Communications

Engineering and Communications Modifications in Civilian and Military Aircraft

Network Operations Center Monitors Communications Around the Globe

ARINC Incorporated was founded in 1929 to provide reliable and efficient radio communications for U.S. airlines. The company moved its headquarters to Annapolis in 1965. Today, ARINC is a $500 million communications and engineering company serving customers around the world. Their 3,000 employees deliver high-quality services and products to three major business areas – civil aviation, national defense and transportation communications.

ARINC's GlobaLink Systems Provide Aviation Communications Worldwide

ARINC develops and operates global communications and information processing systems for customers around the world. These networks allow airlines and air traffic management authorities to stay in touch with aircraft wherever they fly. As part of maintaining worldwide communications, ARINC employees also engineer and integrate new equipment into existing aircraft, both civilian and military, so they may continue to fly while meeting changing flight safety regulations.

159

Maintenance on a C-130J

C-130J Hercules

Pre-Flight Check on a C-130J

A-10 Thunderbolt

The Maryland Air National Guard's 175th Wing operates two of the most versatile aircraft in the U.S. Air Force. The A-10 Thunderbolt jet fighter, a heavily armored light attack bomber, is especially effective against armored vehicles and in missions needing close air support of ground forces. The second aircraft is the C-130 Hercules transport which has participated in military operations around the world. The 175th Wing was the first Air National Guard unit to receive the state-of-the-art C-130J airlifter.

A C-130J Escorted By Two A-10 Thunderbolts

A-10 and C-130 aircraft, of the 175th Wing **Maryland Air National Guard**, grace the sky over Annapolis. Recipients of eight U.S. Air Force Outstanding Unit Awards and numerous flying safety awards, the 175th Wing has missions to work with active duty forces worldwide and to assist State authorities during civil and natural disaster type emergencies. The Maryland Air National Guard, composed of nearly 1700 citizen-airmen, has enjoyed an outstanding relationship with the State of Maryland since 1921.

AH-1 Cobra Attack Helicopter

Cobra Pilots Discuss Strategy

Vehicle with MK-19 Grenade Launcher

TOW Anti-Tank Missile Unit

Maryland Army National Guard's 1st Squadron, 158th Cavalry, is known as "The Governor's Guard," being based in Annapolis at Lt. Col. E. Leslie Medford Armory. As part of one of the U.S. Army's most decorated combat divisions, the 29th Infantry Division (Light), its federal mission is to perform battlefield reconnaissance and security missions. The 158th Cavalry accomplishes this through integrated air-ground combat operations using the AH-1 Cobra attack helicopter and the armored High Mobility Multi-Purpose Wheeled Vehicle equipped with the MK-19 Grenade Launcher, .50 Caliber Machine Gun or the TOW Anti-Tank Missile.

Training with Ground and Air Units

The 158th Cavalry traces its roots as "The Governor's Guard" to 1877 when Annapolis' first militia company was formed. Since then the company has participated in such noted missions as the Meuse-Argonne offensive of WWI and the famed D-Day assault on Normandy in WWII. Today the Maryland Army National Guard employs over 6,400 citizen-soldiers, bringing in more than $130 million in federal funds. The unit's armory recently underwent a major renovation and is available for public use, including a Distance Learning Center where college courses are taught and a telecommunication center for conferences.

Inspecting a Guitar in The Woodshop

Awaiting Final Assembly

The Finish Hall

Body Sanding Area

Paul Reed Smith Guitars produces what many consider to be the finest electric guitars made. Paul created his first guitar as a challenge to a college music professor in exchange for course credit. After that he knew he wanted to make his living building guitars. Starting in a small shop on West Street, above what is now Ram's Head, PRS Guitars has evolved into a 120 employee company. The list of musicians playing PRS guitars is long and notable - a testament to the skill and pride the PRS team puts into every guitar they build.

Film Crew At Work in Annapolis

Maryland Film Office - Behind the scenes - Dominic DeSantis, director of photography, and Lowry Brooks, Jr., writer/producer/director - filming at Annapolis Harbor's famous "Ego Alley". The Maryland Film Office promotes the State of Maryland's diversity of locations for filming by studio-based and independent feature film, television and commercials producers. Members of the film office staff are on call at all times during a production to address the special needs, changes or other requirements that occur during a production.

Looking West from the Severn River, a flotilla of sailboats is backlit as the late afternoon sun streams through a break in the clouds. To quote one enthusiastic Annapolitan, "It is views like this that answer the question of why I want to be here."

DIRECTORY OF FEATURED COMPANIES

ABS - ACTION BUSINESS SYSTEMS
151 West Street, Suite 100   (pg. 154-55)
Annapolis, MD 21401
Phone: 410-224-3333 (Annapolis)
        800-227-6815 (Corp. Headquarters)
Web: www.ABS-TOSHIBA.com

ANNAPOLIS INN   (pg. 49)
144 Prince George Street
Annapolis, MD 21401-1723
Phone: 410-295-5200
Web: www.annapolisinn.com

ANNAPOLIS OPERA, INC.   (pg. 119)
801 Chase Street
Annapolis, MD 21401
Phone: 410-267-8135
Fax: 410-267-6440
Web: www.annapolisopera.com

ANNAPOLIS MARRIOTT WATERFRONT
80 Compromise Street   (pg. 104-05)
Annapolis, MD 21401
Phone: 410-268-7555
Contact: Dana Schuman
Web: www.annapolismarriott.com

ANNAPOLIS SYMPHONY ORCHESTRA
801 Chase Street   (pg. 121)
Annapolis, MD 21401
Phone: 410-263-0907
Web: www.annapolissymphony.org

ANNE ARUNDEL MEDICAL CENTER
2002 Medical Parkway   (pg. 156-57)
Annapolis, MD 21401
Phone: 443-481-1000
Web: www.aahs.org

ARINC, INCORPORATED   (pg. 158-59)
2551 Riva Road
Annapolis, MD 21401
Phone: 410-266-4000
Web: www.arinc.com

BALLET THEATER OF ANNAPOLIS   (pg.120)
801 Chase Street
Annapolis, MD 21401
Phone: 410-263-8289   Fax: 410-626-1835
Web: www.BtaBallet.org

BELKOV YACHT COMPANY   (pg. 144)
311 Third Street
Annapolis, MD 21403
Phone: 410-269-1777

CAPITAL-GAZETTE NEWSPAPERS   (pg. 153)
2000 Capital Drive
Annapolis, MD 21401
Phone: 410-268-5000,   301-261-2200
Web: www.HometownAnnapolis.com

CHART HOUSE   (pg. 108)
300 Second Street
Annapolis, MD 21403
Phone: 410-268-7166 or 410-269-6992
E-mail: annapolis@chart-house.com

FARR® YACHT DESIGN, LTD.   (pg. 140-41)
P.O. Box 4964
613 Third Street, Suite 20
Annapolis, MD 21403-0964
Phone: 410-267-0780   Fax: 410-268-0553
Web: www.farrdesign.com

JOBSON SAILING, INC.   (pg. 137)
Mr. Gary Jobson
3 Church Circle
Annapolis, MD 21401
Phone: 410-263-4630
Web: www.jobsonsailing.com

MARYLAND AIR NATIONAL GUARD
Fifth Regiment Armory   (pg. 160-61)
29th Division Street
Baltimore, MD 21201-2288
Phone: 410-576-6179
Web: www.mdang.ang.af.mil

MARYLAND ARMY NATIONAL GUARD
Fifth Regiment Armory   (pg. 162-63)
29th Division Street
Baltimore, MD 21201-2288
Phone: 410-576-6179 (PAO)
Web: www.marylandguard.com

MARYLAND FILM OFFICE   (pg. 165)
217 E. Redwood Street
Baltimore, MD 21202
Phone: 410-767-6340   Toll Free: 800-333-6632
Web: www.mdfilm.state.md.us

MARYLAND HALL FOR THE ARTS   (pg. 118)
801 Chase Street
Annapolis, MD 21401
Phone: 410-263-5544   Fax: 410-263-5114
Web: www.mdhallarts.org

O'LEARYS SEAFOOD RESTAURANT (pg. 112)
310 Third Street
Annapolis, MD 21403
Phone: 410-263-0884
Web: www.Olearys-Seafood.Com

PAUL REED SMITH GUITARS   (pg. 164)
380 Log Canoe Circle
Stevensville, MD 21666
Phone: 410-643-9970
Web: www.prsguitars.com

PHILLIPS ANNAPOLIS HARBOR RESTAURANT
12 Dock Street - City Dock   (pg. 106)
Annapolis, MD 21401
Phone: 410-990-9888
Corp. Offices: 888-234-CRAB
Web: www.phillipsfoods.com

RUTH'S CHRIS STEAK HOUSE   (pg. 110)
301 Severn Avenue
Annapolis, MD 21403
Phone: 410-990-0033
Web: www.serioussteaks.com

TELECOMMUNICATION SYSTEMS, INC.
275 West Street   (pg. 152)
Annapolis, MD 21401
Phone: 410-263-7616
Fax: 410-263-7617
Web: www.telecomsys.com

UNITED STATES NAVAL ACADEMY (pg. 52)
For information contact:
Armel-Leftwich Visitor Center
U.S. Naval Academy
Annapolis, MD 21402
Phone: 410-293-3363
Web: www.usna.edu

As the morning sun rises over Spa Creek the ducks begin to swim and the boats continue to gently waft in the ebbing tide. So Annapolis begins another spring morning in much the same way it has for over three hundred years. Today, one hears cars in the distance rolling along the streets instead of horses and buggies, and planes pass high overhead. Annapolis is certainly a modern city, yet for everything that has changed there is an equal part which has withstood time. Such is the charm of Anne Arundel Town.